HOT TOPICS

TEENS AND ALCOHOL

A DANGEROUS COMBINATION

By Allison Krumsiek

Portions of this book originally appeared in *Teens and Alcohol* by Michael V. Uschan.

I0869266

LUCENT PRESS

Published in 2019 by
Lucent Press, an Imprint of Greenhaven Publishing, LLC
353 3rd Avenue
Suite 255
New York, NY 10010

Copyright © 2019 Greenhaven Press, a part of Gale, Cengage Learning
Gale and Greenhaven Press are registered trademarks used herein under license.

All new materials copyright © 2019 Lucent Press, an Imprint of Greenhaven Publishing, LLC.

All rights reserved. No part of this book may be reproduced in any form without permission in writing from the publisher, except by a reviewer.

Designer: Deanna Paternostro
Editor: Jennifer Lombardo

Library of Congress Cataloging-in-Publication Data

Names: Krumsiek, Allison, author.
Title: Teens and alcohol : a dangerous combination / by Allison Krumsiek.
Description: New York : Lucent, [2019] | Series: Hot topics | Includes bibliographical references and index.
Identifiers: LCCN 2018017599 (print) | LCCN 2018018419 (ebook) | ISBN 9781534564992 (eBook) | ISBN 9781534564985 (library bound book) | ISBN 9781534564978 (pbk. book)
Subjects: LCSH: Teenagers–Alcohol use–United States–Juvenile literature. | Drinking of alcoholic beverages–United States–Juvenile literature.
Classification: LCC HV5135 (ebook) | LCC HV5135 .K78 2019 (print) | DDC 362.2920835–dc23
LC record available at https://lccn.loc.gov/2018017599

Printed in the United States of America

CPSIA compliance information: Batch #BW19KL: For further information contact Greenhaven Publishing LLC, New York, New York at 1-844-317-7404.

Please visit our website, www.greenhavenpublishing.com. For a free color catalog of all our high-quality books, call toll free 1-844-317-7404 or fax 1-844-317-7405.

CONTENTS

FOREWORD

Adolescence is a time when many people begin to take notice of the world around them. News channels, blogs, and talk radio shows are constantly promoting one view or another; very few are unbiased. Young people also hear conflicting information from parents, friends, teachers, and acquaintances. Often, they will hear only one side of an issue or be given flawed information. People who are trying to support a particular viewpoint may cite inaccurate facts and statistics on their blogs, and news programs present many conflicting views of important issues in our society. In a world where it seems everyone has a platform to share their thoughts, it can be difficult to find unbiased, accurate information about important issues.

It is not only facts that are important. In blog posts, in comments on online videos, and on talk shows, people will share opinions that are not necessarily true or false, but can still have a strong impact. For example, many young people struggle with their body image. Seeing or hearing negative comments about particular body types online can have a huge effect on the way someone views themselves and may lead to depression and anxiety. Although it is important not to keep information hidden from young people under the guise of protecting them, it is equally important to offer encouragement on issues that affect their mental health.

The titles in the Hot Topics series provide readers with different viewpoints on important issues in today's society. Many of these issues, such as domestic abuse and free speech rights online, are of immediate concern to young people. This series aims to give readers factual context on these crucial topics in a way that lets them form their own opinions. The facts presented throughout also serve to empower readers to help themselves or support people they know who are struggling with many of the challenges adolescents face today. Although negative viewpoints are not ignored or downplayed, this series allows young people to see that the challenges they face are not insurmountable. Abusive relationships can be ended, the internet can be navigated safely, and the environment can be saved.

Quotes encompassing all viewpoints are presented and cited so readers can trace them back to their original source, verifying for themselves whether the information comes from a reputable place. Additional books and websites are listed, giving readers a starting point from which to continue their own research. Chapter questions encourage discussion, allowing young people to hear and understand their classmates' points of view as they further solidify their own. Full-color photographs and enlightening charts provide a deeper understanding of the topics at hand. All of these features augment the informative text, helping young people understand the world they live in and formulate their own opinions concerning the best way they can improve it.

"I Paid with the Life of a Good Friend"

A fateful decision to drink and drive ruined the lives of three young men and their community. In the small community of Olney, Maryland, 17-year-old Austin Hall was leaving a party on Labor Day weekend in 2014. Two classmates from Sherwood High School asked for a ride home. Hall, who had been drinking heavily, agreed to drop them off. It was a decision only two of the boys would live to regret.

Neither of the passengers—15-year-old Shawn Gangloff and 17-year-old Max Dechter—had been drinking that night. "He simply chose the wrong person to get a ride home from,"[1] said Gangloff's mother, Allison. Hall sped away from the party at 119 miles (191.5 km) per hour through a neighborhood where the speed limit was 35 miles (56 km) per hour. His car went off the road and hit a light pole. Gangloff, who was not wearing a seatbelt, was thrown from the car during the crash; he was severely injured and died the next day. Dechter was seriously injured; he eventually recovered, but it was a long, difficult process. After the crash, Dechter had to relearn everything from walking to talking to eating on his own. He permanently lost the use of one arm and suffered traumatic brain injury. However, Dechter did not dwell on his own hardships when he spoke at Hall's trial. Instead, he told the court, "I paid with the life of a good friend."[2]

Underage Drinking Dangers

The dangers teens face when they drink have been well documented for years. In 2007, acting U.S. Surgeon General

Kenneth P. Moritsugu issued a report on the scope of underage drinking. The surgeon general, the nation's top public health official, wrote,

> *Underage alcohol consumption in the United States is a widespread and persistent public health and safety problem that creates serious personal, social, and economic consequences for adolescents, their families, communities, and the Nation as a whole. By age 15, approximately 50 percent of boys and girls have had a whole drink of alcohol; by age 21, approximately 90 percent have done so.*[3]

The legal drinking age in all 50 states is 21, which means that the millions of teenagers who drink are breaking the law. Because drinking is illegal for teens, police can arrest them just for possessing alcoholic beverages. School officials can also punish students for drinking even if it did not take place in school. For example, schools often ban athletes from participating in sports if they consume alcohol, and those who post pictures of themselves drinking on social media may find themselves suspended or expelled. While the legality of schools punishing students for off-campus actions has been debated, it has happened more than once. Teenage drinkers can also expect to be disciplined by their parents or guardians.

Teenagers who drink, however, face a much greater risk than being arrested or disciplined by their parents or guardians. A 2006 to 2010 study by the Centers for Disease Control and Prevention (CDC) showed that more than 4,300 young people under the age of 21 die each year as a result of drinking. This 4-year

People who drive drunk risk killing or seriously injuring others. If this happens, they must live with the guilt for the rest of their lives.

study includes an average of 1,580 fatalities in motor vehicle crashes—the leading cause of death among teenagers—as well as other types of accidents. According to the CDC, as of 2016, these numbers have not changed. The most dangerous situation for teens is when they drive or are passengers in cars driven by teens who have been drinking.

However, teens also risk their lives just by drinking alcohol. Their lack of experience with the effects alcohol creates in people can lead them to drink more dangerously than adults. They often are unaware of what their tolerance for alcohol is, and drinking too quickly can cause temporary or permanent damage before they even feel most of the effects. For instance, Molly Ammon, a 19-year-old University of Florida freshman, died from alcohol poisoning in 2011 after drinking heavily at a party in Madeira Beach, Florida. Her blood alcohol concentration (BAC) was 0.408 percent. For comparison, at 0.08 percent, someone can be arrested for driving while intoxicated, and at 0.2 percent, someone often needs help standing up. Excessive drinking is common for teenagers because they tend to drink as much as they can at one time.

The CDC has reported that drinkers between the ages of 12 and 20 consume more than 90 percent of the alcohol they drink during episodes of binge drinking. The National Institute on Alcohol Abuse and Alcoholism (NIAAA) defines binge drinking as five or more drinks (for men) or four or more drinks (for women) within two hours. However, a 2018 study published in the medical journal *The Lancet* found that there is no reason for this

Drinking too much alcohol can lead to life-threatening situations.

difference between the sexes. The study's 120 co-authors, who studied drinking patterns and health outcomes in a group of about 600,000 people from 19 developed countries, suggested that the guidelines should be revised to define moderate drinking as 1 drink per day or 7 per week for both men and women. The researchers found that even at this low level, many people suffered health issues such as heart problems, stroke, and high blood pressure. The more someone drinks, the study found, the lower their life expectancy drops. People who drink 100 grams or less of alcohol per week may live up to five years longer than those who drink 350 grams per week, the study found. Most teens consume more than the minimum amount when they are binge drinking.

In 1992, Joseph A. Califano Jr., a former secretary of the Department of Health, Education, and Welfare—today known as the Department of Health and Human Services—founded the National Center on Addiction and Substance Abuse. An expert on drug abuse, Califano has written and commented extensively on teenage use of alcohol and other drugs. Califano and many others believe alcohol is more dangerous for teens than illegal drugs because it is easier to obtain and is considered socially acceptable; most people do not even consider it a drug, even though it is. This perception of alcohol as a fun, safe substance has caused problems for all drinkers—especially teens.

CHAPTER 1

A Widespread Drug

Alcohol is the most widely used drug in America among all groups, including teens. According to the 2015 National Youth Risk Behavior Survey, 63.2 percent of teens had tried alcohol by the time they reached 12th grade. This is a significant decrease from 81.6 percent in 1991, but it is important to note that 63 percent is still more than half. Most of the respondents of the 2015 survey said they had tried at least 1 alcoholic beverage by 9th grade, and 17 percent of them had done so before age 13. Again, this is down from 1991, when 32.7 percent said they had tried alcohol before age 13. According to the 2015 survey, 32.8 percent of teens said they currently drink alcohol (which the survey defined as having at least 1 drink in the month before they took the survey). This is also down from the 1991 survey, in which 50.8 percent of teens said they currently drink alcohol.

Alcohol use is much more widespread compared to other drugs; for instance, 38.6 percent of teens surveyed for the 2015 report said they had experimented with marijuana by 12th grade. In their book about teenage drug use, Katherine Ketcham and Nicholas A. Pace explained that one reason so many teens try alcohol is that they mistakenly believe it is harmless compared to drugs that are illegal for adults as well as teens. Ketcham and Pace wrote,

> MYTH: *Alcohol isn't really a drug—at least it's not as bad as LSD, cocaine, marijuana, methamphetamines, or heroin.*
>
> FACT: *Alcohol is a toxic, potentially addictive drug that causes more damage to the individual and society than all illegal drugs combined—in fact, alcohol kills ... more young Americans than all illegal drugs combined.*[4]

Current High School Student Alcohol Use

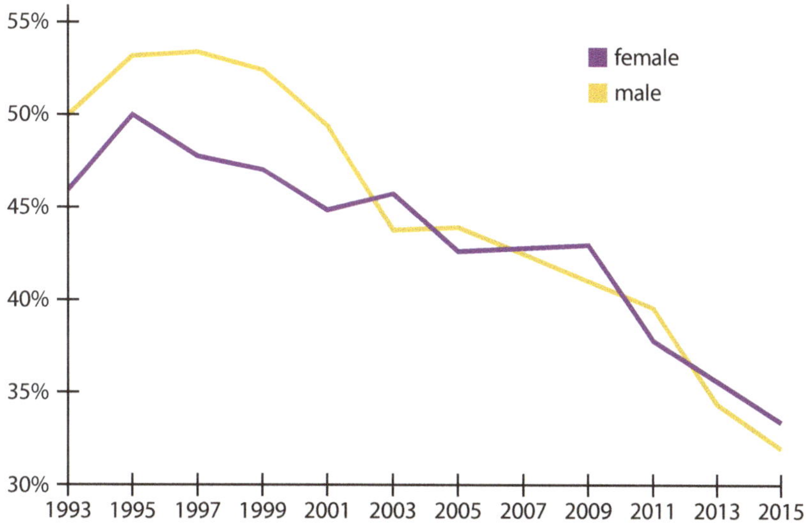

The number of teens who report drinking in high school has decreased dramatically since the 1990s, as this information from the CDC shows, but experts say the number of teen drinkers is still too high.

This claim is backed up by the CDC, whose statistics indicate that 88,000 people die from alcohol-related causes each year, compared to 64,000 deaths from drug overdose. According to *Vox*, these numbers come from an analysis of deaths between 2006 and 2010, which means they may actually have increased in recent years. The dangers alcohol poses to everyone—adults as well as teenagers—include being killed in a drunk driving crash as either a driver or passenger, dying from alcohol poisoning if a person consumes too much during a binge drinking session, and long-term physical and mental damage caused by drinking over time. In addition, alcohol is often cited as a factor in suicides and homicides. It can also lead drinkers to engage in risky behavior that can harm or kill them, such as climbing on top of things while intoxicated, leading them to lose their balance and fall. Because their bodies and brains are not yet fully developed, however, teenage drinkers face several risks that adults do not. Alcohol can damage teenage brains because they are still changing and developing, and people who start drinking in their teens face a higher risk of developing an alcohol use disorder than those who wait to drink until they are older.

Lack of knowledge about the dangers of drinking makes it easy for teenagers to believe alcohol is a harmless substance. However, teenagers also have trouble understanding the dangers of alcohol because of society's nearly universal acceptance of drinking—even heavy drinking. This is especially true if their parents, guardians, or other relatives drink. Many adults downplay drinking; they may joke about silly or dangerous things they did when they were drunk, or claim that it does not matter how many drinks they have at one time as long as they are still in control of their actions. In *A Six-Pack and a Fake I.D.*, Susan and Daniel Cohen explained that the approval society gives to using alcohol makes it hard for teenagers to believe they are doing anything wrong when they drink, even though they are not old enough to do it legally:

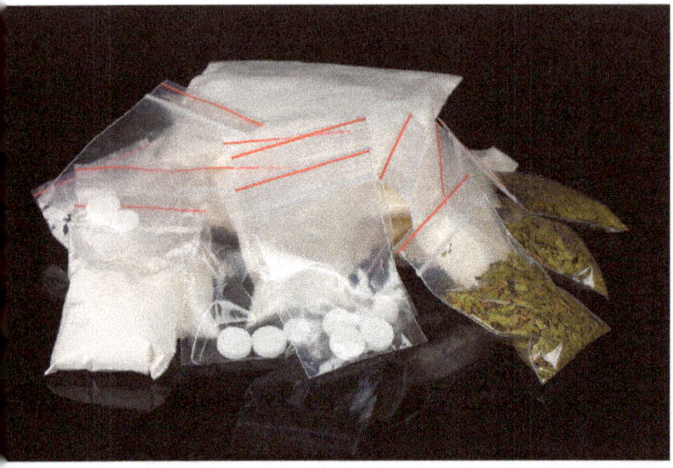

Many people talk about "drugs and alcohol" to distinguish alcohol from illegal drugs such as the ones shown here, but the reality is that alcohol is a drug as well and has the potential to be very dangerous.

> *Alcohol is a drug that is woven into the very fabric of our society. Drinking is part of our history and heritage. It's not going to go away. Since drinking is legal, and what is more important quite acceptable to the vast majority, the social context in which drinking takes place is vastly different from that in which other drugs are used. And that is a vital difference between alcohol and other drugs.*[5]

Society's acceptance of drinking is so strong that Gail Gleason Milgram, an expert on alcohol abuse, wrote, "Alcohol is the drug of choice for most Americans."[6] This attitude toward drinking is rooted in the historic use of alcohol, which extends back thousands of years.

Alcohol: As Old as Time

Ethyl alcohol is the chemical in alcoholic beverages such as beer, wine, and whiskey that intoxicates people. Alcohol is produced by fermentation, which is a chemical reaction that occurs when yeast reacts with food that contains sugar, such as fruits, berries, and grains. Fermentation occurs naturally because yeast can be microscopic and float freely in the air.

No one knows exactly when or how people first discovered how to control the fermentation process. The earliest evidence of alcoholic drinks is from jars found in China that date back to 7000 BC, which means people have been consuming alcoholic beverages for at least 9,000 years. The Chinese jars had traces of an alcoholic beverage made by fermenting rice, honey, and fruit. However, the most widespread early alcoholic drink was beer. Clay tablets found in the ruins of ancient Babylon that are 7,000 years old are the earliest written record that prove people drank beer. Evidence also exists that Egyptians brewed beer thousands of years ago. They called the beverage *hek* and made it by crumbling barley bread into jars, covering it with water, and allowing the yeast in the bread to ferment naturally.

Beer and wine produced through natural fermentation generally have low alcohol contents, about 5 to 8 percent for beer and 12 percent for wine. People living in virtually every part of the world have consumed such drinks for thousands of years. Some historians believe the desire to produce alcohol was one of the reasons early humans started growing wheat; if this is true, it means alcohol has shaped all of human history, causing people to give up their nomadic hunter-gatherer lifestyle and settle in one area.

Brandy, whiskey, and other distilled beverages, which are sometimes called spirits, have a much shorter history. Distillation was discovered first in Arabia in the eighth century and then in Europe in the twelfth century. Distillation produces concentrated alcohol and allows beverages to have alcohol contents ranging from 20 percent to 60 percent, which is far higher than naturally fermented beer and wine. The higher alcohol content in spirits enables people to become drunk by drinking much smaller portions of them than beer or wine.

People have been making beer for thousands of years.

There were many reasons alcoholic beverages became a normal part of everyday life. According to Live Science, people probably started drinking them for purely biological reasons: "The ability to break down alcohol likely helped human ancestors make the most out of rotting, fermented fruit that fell onto the forest floor."[7] However, this biological advantage became unnecessary over time, so it is clear that people continued drinking for other reasons. Many people enjoy consuming alcohol because it can change their mood and potentially make them feel happier. Centuries ago, people also drank alcoholic beverages because so many sources of water and milk were contaminated that people risked getting deadly diseases such as cholera if they consumed them. For example, President Abraham Lincoln's mother died after drinking milk from a cow that had eaten a poisonous weed.

Alcoholic beverages were also an important nutritional source for people with limited diets that were low in calories. This was especially true in Europe, where widespread poverty made it hard for people to buy enough food. In 1551, physician Johann Brettschneider described how average people depended greatly on beer for nourishment: "Some subsist more upon this drink than they do on food … People of both sexes and every age, the hale [healthy] and the infirm [sick] alike require it."[8] Because alcohol has a sedative effect that can ease physical pain from injury, illness, and hard labor, people believed it made them physically stronger, although this was just an illusion. Partially because of this perception, manual laborers drank a lot of beer, especially in England in the 1700s.

In ancient times, alcohol was also used for many medical purposes, such as dressing wounds and fighting fever. The medicinal qualities of wine were held in such high regard that the Talmud, a Jewish religious text, claims, "Wine taken in moderation induces appetites and is beneficial to health. Wine is the greatest of medicines."[9] The Christian Bible's New Testament advises readers to "no longer drink water exclusively, but use a little wine for the sake of your stomach and your frequent ailments."[10] Additionally, in one Bible story, Jesus turns water into wine when the wedding he is attending runs out of it.

As technology has advanced, so has the process of brewing beer.

A Colony of Drink

When English colonists first immigrated to the land that would become the United States, they brought these favorable attitudes about alcohol and drinking traditions with them. On May 14, 1607, the first British colonists established a settlement in Virginia, the first of the colonies that would eventually break away from England and become the United States. Even the Pilgrims, who were very religious, considered alcohol a necessity. Beer was considered vital because in the 17th century, water was often contaminated and could make people sick. Even children drank beer, but its alcohol content was lower than the beer adults drank.

Increase Mather, a prominent minister in Boston, Massachusetts, in the early 1700s, famously stated the positive attitude colonists had toward alcohol when he wrote that it was "the good creature of God [and was] to be received with thankfulness."[11] Alcohol was considered important for social as well as health reasons, and it played an important role in the nation's founding; conversations over mugs of beer and sips of whiskey helped spark the American Revolution. In *The Alcoholic Republic: An American Tradition*, W. J. Rorabaugh wrote,

> *Taverns were … certainly seed beds of the Revolution, the places where British tyranny was condemned, militiamen organized, and independence plotted. Patriots [colonists who opposed British rule] viewed public houses [taverns] as the nurseries of freedom … The British called them public nuisances.*[12]

Residents of the new nation drank even more after the war. Per capita, or per person, annual consumption in the 1830s included 9.5 gallons (35.96 L) of spirits, 1 to 2 gallons of wine (3.8 L to 7.6 L), and 27 gallons (102.2 L) of beer each year. For comparison, the *Huffington Post* reported that in 2010, the average American drank 1.5 gallons (5.7 L) of spirits, 2.3 gallons (8.7 L) of wine, and 20.8 gallons (78.7 L) of beer. Beer was the third most frequently consumed beverage in the United States that year, after soft drinks and bottled water.

History professor Thomas R. Pegram described the lenient attitude toward drinking when the United States was first established:

> *Although community scorn and the power of law was brought to bear on drunkards, everyone was expected to consume alcoholic beverages as dietary staples, and over-indulgence was tolerated at weddings, funerals, militia musters, and on holidays. Women drank in the home; men drank more frequently and more copiously [larger amounts] at home, in the fields or the shop, and at taverns and during public events such as elections; solicitous parents shared beer with children at meals, and encouraged boys to develop a taste for distilled spirits.*[13]

Although people often think of religious people frowning on alcohol, Increase Mather (pictured here) was a preacher who praised it.

The increasingly high drinking levels of many Americans during the 18th and 19th centuries led to

CONSIDERED A SAFE DRINK

"The levels of [alcohol] consumption in colonial America have never been surpassed [by Americans in any other period of its history]; for eighteenth-century Americans alcohol was considered safer and healthier than water."

–James B. Jacobs, author and professor of constitutional law and the courts at New York University

James B. Jacobs, *Drunk Driving: An American Dilemma*. Chicago, IL: University of Chicago Press, 1989, p. 5.

public drunkenness becoming common, incidents of violence, and other social problems. Such alcohol-related problems created a backlash against drinking and spurred attempts to limit and even ban its consumption.

The Prohibition Era

Although most people in the 18th and 19th centuries drank alcoholic beverages at home, many people began drinking in public houses, or pubs—the British name for businesses serving alcohol—for short. Many public houses, which Americans called taverns, saloons, and bars, became centers of criminal activity such as gambling and sex work. Even taverns free of such vices, or wrongdoing, were criticized because their owners encouraged patrons to engage in heavy drinking. There were so many taverns in Philadelphia, Pennsylvania, in 1744 that a grand jury studied the situation. The report claimed the businesses were "little better than Nurseries of Vice and Debauchery, and tend very much to increase the Number of our Poor."[14] Most taverns in Philadelphia were located in a part of the city that became known as Hell Town because of the trouble drunken patrons caused.

In 1826, Presbyterian minister Lyman Beecher helped found the American Temperance Society in Boston. Beecher claimed drinking was dangerous because too many people could not stop once they began: "Much is said about the prudent [sensible] use of spirits, but we might as well speak of the prudent use of the

Alcohol for Strength?

In the 18th and 19th centuries, employers often gave their workers alcoholic beverages during the workday because they believed the energy workers received from the calories in beer and alcohol would make them more productive. Those receiving daily rations of alcohol also included soldiers and sailors. George Washington led colonists to victory during the American Revolution and afterward became the nation's first president. Historian Eric Burns claimed Washington firmly believed alcohol made his soldiers better fighters:

> *During the Revolutionary War, George Washington insisted on alcohol for his men, and once, when a shipment was delayed, he wrote an anguished letter to the president of the Continental Congress: "The benefits arising from the moderate use of strong Liquor," Washington stated, "have been experienced in all Armies and are not to be disputed."*[1]

Today, enough research into alcohol has been done to show that this view is false. Alcohol does not increase strength or productivity, although someone may be strong or productive despite drinking alcohol if they have not had a lot. Most employees and soldiers are no longer given alcohol except on special occasions, such as company parties.

1. Quoted in Eric Burns, *Spirits of America: A Social History of Alcohol*. Philadelphia, PA: Temple University Press, 2004, p. 16.

plague—of fire handed prudently round among [gun]powder—of poison taken prudently every day."[15] Many people, especially those who were tired of the crimes drunk people committed and the amount of household money men spent on alcohol, agreed with Beecher's views, and the temperance movement quickly caught on.

In the second half of the 19th century, more militant groups such as the Anti-Saloon League and the Woman's Christian Temperance Union staged public protests against drinking. The demonstrations sometimes included attacks on saloons by ax-wielding protesters such as Carry Nation, who smashed barrels of beer and whiskey and attacked saloons with her hatchet. In 1846, Maine passed a law prohibiting the sale of alcohol. Concern about the problems drinking caused kept growing, and on January 16, 1919, the nation ratified the 18th Amendment to the Constitution. The amendment prohibited making, transporting, or selling any beverage with more than 0.5 percent alcohol, a level so low that it would not make people drunk.

Bars have existed in the United States since before it was officially a country. Shown here is Lafitte's Blacksmith Shop Bar in New Orleans, Louisiana, which was built between 1722 and 1732. It is believed to be the oldest building used as a bar in what is now the United States; as of 2018, it is still serving alcohol.

Prohibition went into effect on January 16, 1920, but quickly proved to be a failure. Criminals such as Al Capone became millionaires by supplying beer and liquor to people who chose to break the law and drink anyway. The law was so openly ignored and generally hated that in 1933, Congress ratified the 21st Amendment to repeal the 18th. Although Prohibition failed

A NEW VISION FOR SOCIETY

"The reign of tears is over ... The slums will soon be a memory. We will turn our prisons into factories and turn jails into storehouses and corncribs. Men will walk upright now, women will smile and the children will laugh."

–Reverend Billy Sunday's prediction when Prohibition became law

Quoted in Eric Burns, *Spirits of America: A Social History of Alcohol*. Philadelphia, PA: Temple University Press, 2004, p. 187.

nationally, states began more closely regulating the sale and consumption of alcohol.

A FALSE SENSE OF IMPROVEMENT

"Prohibition only drives drunkenness behind doors and into dark places, and does not cure or even diminish it."

–author Mark Twain, who did not live to see Prohibition but firmly believed any attempt to stop people from drinking would fail

Quoted in Paul Sann, *The Lawless Decade: A Pictorial History of a Great American Transition: From the World War I Armistice and Prohibition to Repeal and the New Deal*. New York, NY: Bonanza, 1957, p. 92.

Alcohol and Youth

Until Prohibition, there had been few restrictions on drinking and no age limits, which meant teenagers could drink. This was partly because until the 20th century, many teens began working, marrying, and leaving home to live alone at earlier ages than today. When Prohibition ended in 1933, most states set the drinking age at 21, which was also the voting age at the time. There were some exceptions: Ohio set the drinking age at 16 before raising it to 18 in 1935, and Wisconsin and a few other states allowed 18-year-olds to drink beer. The differing drinking ages in neighboring states sometimes led young people to cross state lines to drink. In states that border Canada, where the drinking age is 18 or 19 depending on the province, they would often also cross the international border. This is still common practice today. However, if no one was appointed to be the designated driver, the risk of getting into a serious crash increased because of how far they had to drive home.

The nation's involvement in the Vietnam War in the 1960s led the country to lower the voting age from 21 to 18 in 1971. That was because so many young men ages 18 to 20 were fighting and dying for their country but could not vote on the policies that had led to war. The same reasoning led about 26 states to lower their drinking ages to 18 as well. These laws were passed between 1969 and 1976. Alex Wagenaar, a University of Florida professor who is an expert on alcohol-related issues, explained, "The argument became: If 18-year-olds can fight and vote, then they should be able to have a drink."[16] The decision to allow teens to drink, however, proved disastrous.

Between 1970 and 1975, there was a 15 to 20 percent increase in alcohol-related automobile accidents involving teenagers, and the estimated number of teens who died in such crashes rose from 7,797 to nearly 9,000. A 2014 study found similar results, proving that this was not a coincidence. Dr. Russell Callaghan studied young Canadian men and found that "when compared to Canadian males slightly younger than the minimum legal drinking age, young men who are just older than the drinking age have significant and abrupt increases in mortality, especially from injuries and motor vehicle accidents."[17]

The 18th Amendment Lives On

The 18th Amendment banning the sale and consumption of alcoholic beverages went into effect on January 16, 1920, and lasted until December 5, 1933, when the 21st Amendment repealed it. Prohibition drastically reduced alcohol consumption, but millions of Americans continued to drink despite the fact that it was illegal. Often they would make their own alcohol, which was sometimes strong enough to cause blindness or death. Even though Prohibition is considered a failed experiment because it did not last, historian Robert Kelley claimed Prohibition had some beneficial effects. For instance, Kelley wrote, Prohibition changed the nation's drinking habits:

> *Cheap liquor would never be available again so readily as in the past. Drinking to excess in public, so common before Prohibition, had lost much of its macho appeal. [And a new] general ethic of moderation in drinking would mean that repeal, when it finally came in 1933, would see not a revival of the old, but entry into a new national relationship with alcohol.*[1]

1. Robert Kelley, *The Shaping of the American Past: 1865 to Present*. Englewood Cliffs, NJ: Prentice Hall, 1990, p. 576.

The drinking age was lowered in many states in the early 1970s after the voting age was lowered. Eighteen-year-old soldiers protested that if they were old enough to fight, they were old enough to vote and drink.

The increased danger to teens led 11 states to raise their drinking ages again after 1975. However, the actions by those states to protect teenagers did not completely solve the problem. Again, many teens simply drove across state or national lines to drink in places where the age was lower. In the end, it would require action by the federal government to reduce the number of teenage drunk drivers.

Congress Acts Again

In 1982, President Ronald Reagan established a commission to study the nation's drunk driving problem. On April 5, 1983, Reagan said the commission had formulated 39 proposals to reduce drunk driving, one of which was to establish a nationwide drinking age of 21. Reagan said, "Because of the correlation between the number of drunk driving fatalities and liberal drinking-age laws, the Commission has recommended that every State set

VIEWING ALCOHOL AS EVIL

"Spirits ... impair the memory, debilitate the understanding, and pervert the moral faculties ... They produce not only falsehood, but fraud, theft, uncleanliness, and murder."

–Benjamin Rush, one of the signers of the Declaration of Independence

Quoted in C. Furnas, *The Life and Times of the Late Demon Rum*. New York, NY: Putnam's Sons, 1965, p. 111.

twenty-one as the minimum legal age for drinking alcoholic beverages."[18] On July 17, 1984, Congress passed the National Minimum Drinking Age Act to require all states to make 21 the minimum age for purchasing and publicly possessing alcoholic beverages. The act was not mandatory. As a threat to make states honor the law, the government said it would reduce federal highway funds by 5 percent for any state that did not increase the drinking age by October 1, 1986.

Many businesses that sell alcohol post signs similar to this one. The business owners and employees face harsh legal penalties and fines if they sell to minors, so to be safe, they generally require an ID from everyone.

Most states immediately changed their legal drinking age to 21. In January 1985, governors from six northeastern states met in Danbury, Connecticut, and committed themselves to honoring the federal law. Mario Cuomo, who was governor of New York at the time, explained why he believed a higher drinking age was necessary: "We have people pouring over the borders now from Pennsylvania and the other states [where the age already was 21] coming to us to get a drink because we have 19 [set as the drinking age]. That's causing deaths and injury."[19] Although some states were reluctant to make the change, by 1988, all 50 states had complied with the law and increased their drinking age to 21.

Current Attitudes Toward Drinking

Attitudes toward alcohol have varied depending on the historical era as well as geographical location. For instance, in the United States in the 1950s and 1960s, it was considered acceptable for a high-ranking businessman to have spirits in his office and to have a drink (or several) at lunch and throughout the workday. This can be seen on the popular TV show *Mad Men*, which aired from 2007 to 2015, although it is likely real workers drank much less than the show's characters did. Over time, this culture changed, and now most people in the United States consider it very inappropriate for an employee to have a drink at all during the workday, even if they are not actually working. Even drinking off-site on a lunch break could be against a company's policy due to concerns about the employee's safety and performance. At best, someone will likely get disapproval from their coworkers or bosses, and at worst, they could be fired. Some companies do allow their employees to drink during the workday, but these are the exception, not a normal occurrence.

In contrast, drinking during the workday is generally considered acceptable in many other countries, especially European ones. Employees may go to lunch and have one or two drinks; for many adults, especially those who drink regularly, this is not enough alcohol to impair their work performance. Additionally, some Europeans have a drink in the morning, which is often considered a sign of alcoholic behavior in the United States. The difference in these cultural attitudes likely has several different factors, one of which may be the fact that European countries have not had an era of Prohibition during which alcohol was blamed for most social evils.

American views toward alcohol tend to be split a bit confusingly. While many people agree that drinking during a workday is unacceptable in most circumstances, the same people often drink enthusiastically on evenings and weekends, and sometimes even in the morning on certain occasions, such as holidays, at brunch, or at parties. Certain drinks, too, are seen as acceptable or unacceptable, although there is no clear reason why this might be so. For instance, a Bloody Mary, which is a cocktail made with vodka and tomato juice, is considered an acceptable brunch drink, but vodka that is not mixed into a cocktail is generally considered socially unacceptable during the day.

However, for many adults, alcohol in general is seen as something that enhances a social situation and makes it more fun. Weddings with open bars (where the alcohol is free for guests and they can drink as much as they like) are seen as better than weddings with cash bars (where guests pay for each drink, as at a regular bar, which limits their drinking to how much they can afford); parties often have a ready supply of alcohol,

Brunch is one of the few occasions where it is considered socially acceptable to drink during the day. People often have mimosas, a drink made with orange juice and champagne.

and people may volunteer to go on "beer runs" if the drinks run out before the guests are ready to leave; and wine in particular is seen as an important part of a girls' night or after-work relaxation ritual. This is reinforced in TV shows, movies, and music as well as the many items—including signs, T-shirts, and drinking glasses—that are sold with slogans on them such as "Wine is cheaper than therapy" and "Coffee keeps me going until it's time for wine." This combination of the glorification of alcohol and strict adherence to the 21-year-old drinking age in the United States has a dangerous effect on many teens. They tend to see it as a forbidden but essential pleasure, leading them to overindulge when they have a chance to drink; many people are well into their 20s or 30s before they lose this mentality, and some never lose it at all. According to the website Choose Responsibility,

> *[T]he World Health Organization found that in many European countries where the drinking age is 18 or younger (and often not enforced), 15- and 16-year-old teens have more drinking occasions per month, but fewer occasions of dangerous intoxication than their American counterparts. In many southern European countries roughly one in ten of all drinking occasions results in intoxication, while in the United States almost half of all drinking occasions result in intoxication. In these countries the introduction of alcohol typically comes from parents. In the United States, where the drinking age is 21, parents are not legally afforded that opportunity, and as a result initiation to alcohol consumption is not responsibly controlled.*[20]

CHAPTER 2

Why People Drink

Actress and singer Demi Lovato has been open with her fans about her struggles with many things. Her biggest struggle early on was with alcoholism and addiction. "I was going to the airport and I had a Sprite bottle just filled with vodka and it was just nine in the morning and I was throwing up in the car," she said. "I think at 19 years old, I had a moment where I was like, 'Oh my God … that is alcoholic behavior. [It's] no longer, I'm young and rebellious and out having fun, it was, wow, I'm one of those people … I gotta get [it] together.'"[21]

Lovato's addictions began as a way to hide her emotions and deal with depression and an eating disorder. Celebrities are not the only ones who start drinking to cover up other problems. The reasons teens start drinking alcohol are as varied as each one's personality. Some drink to feel happier or more social, some to cover up emotional problems, and some to conform to peer pressure. No matter why teens start using alcohol, the results can be permanently damaging.

Demi Lovato struggled with an alcohol use disorder when she was a teenager.

"But Everyone Does It"

In *A Six-Pack and a Fake I.D.*, Susan and Daniel Cohen wrote that most young people will drink alcohol for the first time before they turn 21. They claim teenage drinking is so widespread that teens consider it an ordinary activity, one that they and most of their friends feel they have a right to do even though it is illegal:

Drinking—it's a fact of life that you confront in your teen years. You may consider drinking a pleasure, a right, and a social necessity. Your parents, your school, and the over twenty-one world in general may consider your drinking a problem—and they have made it illegal to boot. But you're not going to let that stop you![22]

It is hard for many teenagers to believe they are doing anything wrong because in a few years, they will be able to drink legally. The fact that many adults in their lives drink alcohol also makes them question why they cannot. It is especially hard for teenagers to think drinking is wrong if their parents or close relatives are heavy drinkers. One recovering alcoholic wrote online that his father accidentally conditioned him to believe drinking was a good thing by giving him sips of beer when he was a small child. He wrote that because "my father was always 'happy' when he was drinking [I] quickly equated drinking with happiness."[23]

NOT EVERYONE SHOULD

"Because I can't do it responsibly. Because one drink doesn't relax me; it only energizes me and makes me want more. Because I can't get out of my own way if I drink. Because my life is better sober. Because, towards the end of my drinking, I didn't have a life anymore."

–author Anna David, who began drinking at age 12, explains why she quit

Quoted in Caren Osten Gerszberg, "Interview with Anna David, Author of the Memoir 'Falling for Me,'" *Drinking Diaries: From Celebration to Revelation*, October 12, 2011. www.drinkingdiaries.com/2011/10/12/interview-with-anna-david-author-of.

Teenagers also have a difficult time rejecting drinking because they are bombarded daily with TV commercials, online ads, and billboards proclaiming the virtues of various brands of alcohol. The media reinforces their belief that drinking is normal. James B. Jacobs, a law professor who has studied the drunk driving problem in the United States, is the author of the book *Drunk Driving: An American Dilemma*. In his book, Jacobs claims that society's overwhelming acceptance of alcohol is one reason

Ads for alcohol can be seen in many public places.

why so many people drink, teens and adults alike. Jacobs also explains that the reasons people start drinking, and then often find it hard to stop, are due to the way alcohol affects people psychologically and emotionally:

> *Drinkers seek reduction of tension, guilt, anxiety, and frustration. From personal experience and from viewing countless television and movie dramas, we have become accustomed to people turning to alcohol to cope with a hard day, family problems, or bad news. People also imbibe [drink] alcohol to loosen up, let down their hair, release inhibitions … [They] also turn to alcohol to fortify confidence, enhance self-esteem, and increase aggressiveness.*[24]

The basic psychological and emotional benefits people seek when they drink are common to both teenagers and adults. However, teenagers have their own unique sets of circumstances that can push them toward taking that first sip of alcohol. One of the most powerful is that they are trying to leave childhood behind and gain what they perceive as the superior status of being an adult.

A Society of Pressured Drinking

Toren Volkmann did not start drinking heavily until he went to college; when that happened, he could not stop and became an alcoholic. After Volkmann managed to quit, he and his mother, Chris, wrote a book about his descent into alcoholism. Volkmann has spoken about why he believes so many young people start drinking: "I think teenagers view alcohol—and I

Pressure for Teens to Drink

Teenagers have many and varied reasons for drinking. In *Teens Under the Influence*, Katherine Ketcham and Nicholas A. Pace list some of the reasons why teenagers drink and use other drugs:

> *Many kids use drugs for the same general reasons adults use drugs–to get high, to feel happy, stimulated, relaxed, or intoxicated; to ease stress, frustration, tension, disappointment, fear, or anger; to take their minds off their pain or their troubles.*
>
> *Kids may start drinking or using other drugs to impress their friends, to rebel against their parents or society, or because they don't want to be seen as preppies or suck-ups …*
>
> *[They may drink] to fit in, or to avoid drawing attention to themselves. If they belong to a gang, they may use drugs to win respect, be cool, or just because that's what everyone else is doing …*
>
> *[Teens] who are anxious or fearful may use alcohol and/or other drugs to boost their self-confidence. Extroverted, outgoing teenagers may use drugs because they like the company of other fun-loving, risk-taking kids.*[1]

1. Katherine Ketcham and Nicholas A. Pace, *Teens Under the Influence: The Truth About Kids, Alcohol and Other Drugs–How to Recognize the Problem and What to Do About It*. New York, NY: Ballantine, 2003, p. 25.

certainly did—as something that's very glamorous."[25] The powerful attraction teenagers have to alcohol and the almost magical qualities they feel it will endow them with are strongly rooted in their desire to become adults.

Teenagers often feel trapped between childhood and adulthood. Drinking is something they cannot legally do until they are older, so many believe that having that first drink becomes a rite of passage to adulthood, similar to getting a driver's license, going to college, or working to support themselves. Movies and other

In the movie Superbad, *the main characters (shown here) view getting drunk as a way for them to have a good time and become respected by their peers.*

media make drinking look fun and harmless: From classic movies such as 1984's *Sixteen Candles* to modern ones such as 2012's *Project X*, Hollywood often portrays getting drunk as a way to bond with peers and have a good time.

An equally powerful reason why teenagers start drinking is peer pressure. Alexandra Robbins wrote *The Geeks Shall Inherit the Earth*, a book that explains why some people who are not popular in high school become successful as adults. Robbins interviewed many young people about their fierce desire to be popular. She said in an interview that peer pressure to conform to accepted standards of conduct among fellow students leads many young people to start drinking so they will be accepted and respected:

> *Many surveys report that the average age students begin drinking is about 14. Many students told me that they start to feel pressure to drink in seventh grade. Anecdotally, teens say that they drink to have fun and to let off steam, but mostly to fit in. They think that everyone else is drinking, so they figure they have to conform. Also, they want to prove that there's "more to them" than what classmates see at school. They figure if they drink, that proves that they can party.*[26]

The same need to fit in and be liked can also lead older teenagers to start drinking. It happened to Volkmann when he left home to attend college: "At college, you'll encounter a whole new group of people, many of [whom] drink regularly. I got sucked into that very lifestyle, and after a while, I found it did me no good. There is so much pressure to drink not only from your friends, but to just fit in when you go off to college."[27]

Alcohol's Effects on Emotions

Another reason why people like to drink is because of the powerful effect it has on their emotions. Behavioral psychologist Reid K. Hester, who has studied the effects of alcohol on teens, explained how alcohol can affect people: "Alcohol is a powerful drug and changes how you feel. Some of the initial sensations at lower blood alcohol levels are pleasant and it is this sensation that many teens, as well as adults, seek."[28] Some of these pleasant sensations include feelings of relaxation and happiness, increased sociability, and a slight feeling of lightheadedness that many people enjoy. According to a 2012 study by researchers at the University of Illinois at Chicago, a BAC of 0.075 can help people find creative solutions to problems because it allows their minds to wander in directions they might not have thought of otherwise.

Although these effects are real, they are often magnified by people's minds. This can be seen in the TV show *The Big Bang Theory*. In the early seasons, the character Raj is too shy to speak to women unless he has been drinking. In some cases, all he needs is one sip of a drink, and the effects can be seen immediately. Such a small amount of alcohol would have no effect on the body and would not be felt that quickly even if it did, proving that the effects are psychosomatic, or all in his head. This is pointed out by the other characters in one episode where Raj does not realize he has been drinking non-alcoholic beer. In real life, some people behave

For the first few seasons of The Big Bang Theory, *Raj (left) felt unable to talk to women unless he had been drinking. This was revealed to be because of his view about how alcohol would make him feel rather than because of its true effects.*

FILLING A HOLE

"I don't know why I did it ... It wasn't peer pressure ... a lot of my friends don't drink at all. My parents don't drink ... Maybe I was bored. It was a small town, and it seemed like there wasn't anything else to do."

–Michelle, who began drinking heavily on weekends at age 18

Quoted in Barbara Strauch, *The Primal Teen: What the New Discoveries About the Teenage Brain Tell Us About Our Kids*. New York, NY: Doubleday, 2003, p. 174.

the same way; because they expect to feel the effects of alcohol, they believe they are feeling them much more quickly than is physically possible. This can create an overreliance on alcohol in social situations.

Teenagers are especially vulnerable to wanting to feel better, or at least different, because of the tremendous changes taking place in their lives, including the anxieties of dating and learning to socialize with other young people. Jeff drank for the first time at age 13 when he took a bottle of his father's liquor and shared it with a friend. He said he learned to like drinking because it made him feel good and made him more comfortable in social situations: "All my anxiety and shyness left and I could talk to girls and other people and dance at parties with no nervousness. It definitely helped me feel more at ease. I was more outgoing when drinking. I did start going to more parties when drinking because I was socially more comfortable when drunk."[29]

Even when people have bad experiences with alcohol, they often keep drinking. Wendy had her first drink when she was 12, and her first heavy drinking experience came a year later during her first date when she went to a dance. When other students passed around a bottle of whiskey, she drank so much that she became violently ill. However, Wendy liked how alcohol made her feel and continued drinking despite that first awful experience.

Being more comfortable socially is one of the many reasons teens drink. Another reason is to ease their emotional turmoil

Drinking too much can cause people to vomit. However, many teens continue to drink even after having this negative experience multiple times.

over a wide range of problems. For instance, anger motivated John to begin drinking at age 15. The death of his grandfather, whom he was very close to, made him so angry that he began drinking to feel better. In another instance, Amanda Welch said she and her sister Liz, coauthors of the book *The Kids Are All Right*, turned to alcohol in their teens to relieve their depression after their mother died. The emotional changes alcohol creates in drinkers is this powerful drug's main attraction. Alcohol can make people feel different because of the way it works in their bodies.

Balancing Good and Bad

In a book on alcoholism, James R. Milam and Katherine Ketcham wrote, "Alcohol is an infinitely confusing substance. In small amounts it is an exhilarating stimulant. In larger amounts it acts as a sedative and as a toxic, or poisonous, agent. When taken in very large amounts over long periods of time [it] can be damaging to cells, tissues, and organs."[30]

AN ALCOHOLIC AT 14

"I was a big drinker at the time. I would drink every day. I would drink alone. I thought the whole concept was so … cool … I knew it was a problem when I liked it more than I liked doing anything else … Like, at first it's fine and you think you have a dark side–it's exciting–and then you realise the dark side wins every time if you decide to indulge in it … It was the worst thing that ever happened to me."

–Lana Del Rey, singer

Quoted in Jamie Crossan, "Lana Del Rey: 'I Was Sent to Boarding School Age 14 to Get Sober,'" NME.com, September 8, 2012. www.nme.com/news/music/lana-del-rey-149-1264690

When people drink, their bodies begin absorbing alcohol immediately—5 to 10 percent of alcohol is transferred to the bloodstream directly through the lining of the mouth. In a 2012 study that was published in the journal *Wine Studies*, researchers found that when participants swished 0.5 ounce (15 mL) each of 10 wine samples and then spit the wine out, their BAC was raised to 0.0026 percent. While this is incredibly low, it shows that some alcohol can be absorbed even if the person does not swallow their drink.

Of course, even more alcohol is absorbed when the person does swallow and the alcohol reaches the stomach and small intestine. The first small doses of alcohol increase blood flow, accelerate the heart rate, and stimulate brain cells to speed up the transmission of nerve impulses. This is due to the calories alcohol contains, which makes the body react the same way it does when someone eats food. Those simple physical changes can ease emotional tension and make people feel happier. Alcohol also makes people feel good because small doses of it boost levels of dopamine, a neurotransmitter in the brain related to pleasant sensations.

However, the effects alcohol has on people change as they continue drinking. Although alcohol can make people feel energized, it is actually a powerful central nervous system depressant, one that is generally classified with drugs such as barbiturates, minor tranquilizers, and general anesthetics. As a depressant, alcohol depresses, or slows down, operation of the central nervous system, which includes the brain and the spinal cord. Depressed performance of the central nervous system from alcohol consumption creates the slurred speech, impaired physical coordination, and other physical and mental symptoms of intoxication.

A standard drink is defined as one that contains 0.5 ounce (15 mL) of alcohol. Because of their varying alcohol contents, that amount of alcohol is found in 12 ounces (354 mL) of beer, 5 ounces (148 mL) of wine, or 1.5 ounces (44 mL) of 80-proof distilled spirits such as whiskey or vodka. Proof measures how much of the liquid in the bottle is pure alcohol—the proof number is simply double the percentage, which means an

The shape and size of a glass can make it difficult for someone to estimate how much they are drinking because different glasses hold different amounts of liquid.

80-proof spirit is made up of 40 percent alcohol. However, most people do not measure their drinks, so they are frequently drinking more than they realize, especially when considering distilled spirits with a high proof number. For instance, wineglasses come in different sizes and shapes, and it can be difficult for someone to estimate how much they hold just by looking at them. Additionally, people tend to fill their glasses nearly to the top. In a wineglass that holds 5 ounces (148 mL), this is about 1 drink, but in a wineglass that holds 21 ounces (621 mL), it is about 4 drinks. However, most people think of both of these as one drink because they are not refilling their glass. This can cause someone to get much more intoxicated than they intended to.

The human body can process alcohol at a fixed rate of one standard drink per hour, so people who consume more than one drink per hour will have increasingly high levels of alcohol in their blood. A BAC of 0.10 percent means a person's bloodstream has 1 part alcohol per 1,000 parts of blood. A BAC of 0.08 percent is legal proof in every state that a person is drunk, although the effects start becoming noticeable at 0.02 percent. Someone who is caught driving with a BAC of 0.08 or more can be arrested and charged with a DUI or DWI (driving under the influence or driving while intoxicated). This is often simply called "drunk driving." However, numerous studies have shown that "buzzed driving," which is when a person has a BAC of less

Many people drink beer by the pint, which is 16 ounces (473 mL), but 1 drink is defined as 12 ounces (354 mL).

than 0.08, is just as dangerous even if it does not have legal repercussions for adults.

People become intoxicated because alcohol affects their brain, which controls their physical functioning as well as their emotions. The speed and severity with which people become intoxicated depends on several factors besides how much alcohol they drink or how fast they consume it. One is the size of the drinker. Someone weighing 250 pounds (113.4 kg) will not become as intoxicated by the same amount of alcohol as someone weighing 125 pounds (56.7 kg); their blood supply is correspondingly larger, so their BAC will not rise as rapidly as that of a smaller person drinking the same amount of alcohol. People who have eaten recently or eat while they drink absorb alcohol more slowly because their body is absorbing food as well as alcohol. Women generally metabolize alcohol more quickly than men, which means they can become intoxicated more quickly. Some people are also able to drink more without being affected by alcohol because of their unique body chemistry.

Teenagers are more susceptible to the effects of alcohol if they are drinking for the first time or have not drunk alcohol very often. They tend to overestimate the amount of alcohol their body can handle, which increases the risk that they will drink too much. People who drink regularly develop a tolerance for alcohol that lessens its effects on them, but if they stop for awhile, this tolerance decreases, so they share the same risk if they start again—even more so, in fact, because they remember what their limit used to be and are generally unaware that it has changed.

An Altered State

BAC levels determine how drunk someone is. As BAC increases, so do the symptoms of intoxication. The effects begin at as low as 0.02 percent, but they are generally not noticeable to others. At 0.04 percent someone may describe themselves as "tipsy," showing very slight changes such as increased sociability. When BAC reaches 0.07 to 0.09 percent, someone is legally considered drunk. At this level, people experience mild "impairment of balance, speech, vision, reaction time, and hearing ... Judgment and self-control are reduced, and caution, reason and memory

It Starts in the Brain

Many people drink alcohol because it makes them feel good. When their bloodstream channels alcohol to the brain, it affects the nucleus accumbens. This specialized part of the brain is the seat of emotion and pleasure that is responsible for feelings of gratification, such as when people eat to satisfy hunger. When alcohol and other addictive drugs hit the brain, the nucleus accumbens releases dopamine, which produces feelings ranging from mild happiness to euphoria. *Newsweek* explained how this works:

> *[Dopamine] produces a feel-good sensation. Eating cheesecake or tacos or any other food you love activates it. So does … winning a competition, acing a test, receiving praise and other pleasurable experiences. The pleasure circuit communicates in the chemical language of dopamine: this neurotransmitter zips from neuron to neuron in the circuit like a molecular happy face …*
>
> *"Drugs of abuse increase the concentration of dopamine in the brain's reward circuits," says Nora Volkow of Brookhaven National Lab. The drugs do that more intensely than any mere behavior, be it eating a four-star meal or winning the lottery.*[1]

1. *Newsweek* Staff, "How It All Starts in Your Brain," *Newsweek*, February 12, 2001. www.newsweek.com/how-it-all-starts-inside-your-brain-155189.

are impaired."[31] As BAC rises, these effects get stronger. By about 0.14 percent, someone may have difficulty seeing or standing; by 0.2 percent, people often throw up, lose awareness of what is going on around them (a state known as a blackout), and risk seriously injuring themselves because they feel less pain and are therefore unaware they are injured; 0.35 percent "is the level of surgical anesthesia,"[32] so someone may fall into a coma; and 0.4 percent is likely to cause death or permanent bodily damage.

At its highest levels, alcohol acts as a poison that can kill drinkers by depressing their brain activity so much that they

A high BAC makes it difficult for people to keep their balance. This can lead to accidents that cause injury or death.

stop breathing. This form of death is known as alcohol poisoning, and it can happen because alcohol affects the brain more strongly than any other part of the body.

Alcohol affects not only how the brain controls the body physically but also how the drinker will react mentally and emotionally. This impairment can sneak up on people because after the first couple of drinks, "an illusion may be created of clarity of mind and thought."[33] Since people feel good, they keep drinking, even though they start to feel worse after a few more drinks.

Higher levels of alcohol can cause emotional changes in drinkers, including making them angry over small things, which is why fights in bars are common. Alcohol also reduces natural inhibitions that keep people from doing dangerous or foolish things. It is important to note that alcohol does not change who a person is. In many cases, it just helps them overcome the restraints that might normally keep them from acting on their desires. These include fear of physical or social consequences as well as fear of judgment from others. For instance, someone who cheats on their partner while they are drunk has likely thought about cheating when they are sober but may not have done so out of concern for how their partner or friends might react. These lapses in judgment happen because large amounts of alcohol destroy people's ability to understand what is happening to them physically, intellectually, and emotionally.

One of the effects of drinking too much is that intoxicated people generally do not realize how alcohol has affected them. To prove this, BuzzFeed's Try Guys did an informal experiment that involved a night of drinking. At various points throughout the evening, they performed a round of tests. After each drink they took together, they tried dancing; having a conversation with someone else at the party; and performing a field sobriety test, which included things such as attempting to walk in a straight line and taking a Breathalyzer test.

As the night went on, they made guesses about how drunk they were based on how they performed the first two tests, but they were frequently surprised by the results of their Breathalyzer tests. For instance, after the second round, Keith was shocked to find that his BAC was 0.049 percent, meaning he was not legally considered drunk. Eugene commented, "You're not legally drunk until actually way later than we thought."[34] Keith and Ned—whose BAC at that point was even lower than Keith's—both agreed they would not feel comfortable driving a car at that level, based on the way they felt physically. About 15 minutes after that point, Keith tried the Breathalyzer again and the result was 0.067. He noted, "So you could … leave a place at 0.06 but you could totally be driving at 0.09, and you would think you were okay … I didn't realize how many drinks it took to get to 0.08 or how … just sitting, you could get drunker."[35] Eugene, who described himself at the beginning of the video as a heavy drinker, said at the end of the night that he did not feel very drunk even after his BAC reached 0.095; he explained, "You don't necessarily have a lower blood alcohol content level because you can drink more, because you don't feel as drunk; you will still be arrested."[36] However, for young adults, drinking has more long-term effects than just being arrested.

The Try Guys are known, as their name suggests, for trying new things and doing informal experiments. From left to right, they are Eugene, Zach, Ned, and Keith.

CHAPTER 3

The Dangers of Underage Drinking

Many teens are drawn to alcohol because of a combination of external and internal factors. Their bodies and brains are still developing, so they feel emotions more deeply. They are also more likely to take risks because it is harder for their brains to assess consequences. This can be exacerbated, or made worse, if they have a disorder such as attention-deficit/hyperactivity disorder (ADHD) or bipolar disorder. "I can't think of a more challenging period of development," said B. J. Casey, a psychology professor at Yale University in New Haven, Connecticut. "Every time I give a talk, I ask people to raise their hand if they want to go through adolescence again. And no one does."[37]

Unfortunately, the fact that a teen's brain is still developing not only makes them more likely to drink, it also makes them more likely to sustain damage from alcohol, even if they do not drink a lot. The effects of alcohol are not confined to the time people are physically drinking. Alcohol dehydrates the body, so people who drink too much alcohol and not enough water experience a hangover the next day. Symptoms can include tiredness, headache, nausea, vomiting, shakiness, and decreased ability to concentrate. Being hungover can negatively affect a person's performance at work or in school, and if someone drinks a large enough amount the night before, the hangover symptoms can be severe enough to keep them home sick. So even if someone is only drinking at night, they may have trouble keeping up with their daytime activities.

Drinking heavily over a long period of time can also lead to serious long-term health risks—most notably, liver disease. Because alcohol is processed in the liver, too much of it can irreversibly damage this organ, causing problems such as fatty liver (too much fat in the liver), alcoholic hepatitis (inflammation of the liver), and cirrhosis (when scar tissue replaces liver tissue, impairing the liver's function). Cirrhosis is the most serious; it cannot be reversed, and it can be deadly. People who have this disease may not know it for a long time because there are often no symptoms. Those who have been drinking more than 3 ounces (89 mL) of alcohol—about 6 cans of beer, 5 glasses of wine, or 6 shots of liquor—per day for more than 8 years are likely to develop cirrhosis. This means that someone who starts drinking heavily at age 14 could develop cirrhosis by as early as age 22. Excessive alcohol use can cause other problems as well, such as an increased risk of breast cancer, heart disease, and stroke.

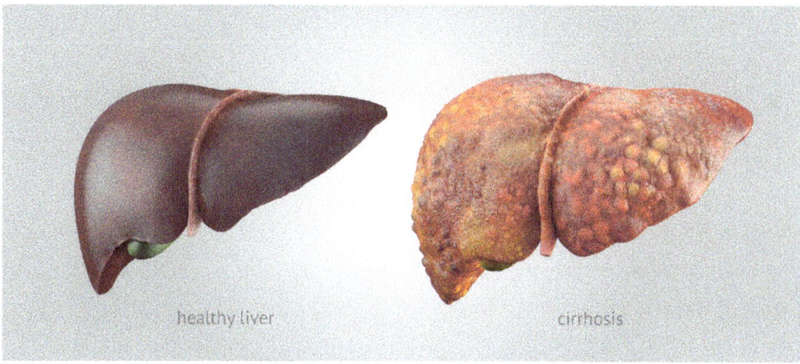

Over time, heavy drinking can cause a condition known as cirrhosis of the liver, in which healthy tissue is replaced with scar tissue. This causes the liver to stop working.

Teen Drinking and Driving

The negative effects of alcohol extend beyond a person's individual health risks. Although liver damage may kill someone slowly, someone who decides to drink and drive has a high chance of dying suddenly. Even when teenage drivers have not been drinking, they pose more of a danger to themselves and their passengers than older drivers because teenagers in general are involved in so many accidents. In 2015, 6 people between the ages of 16 and 19 died every day from motor vehicle injuries, and statistics showed that for every mile teens drove, they were 4 times more likely than older drivers to be involved in a collision.

MULTIPLE NEGATIVE EFFECTS

"Alcohol damages the young brain, interferes with mental and social development, and interrupts academic progress. Alcohol is ... a major factor in the three leading causes of teen death–accidents, homicide, and suicide."

–Joseph A. Califano Jr., founder of the National Center on Addiction and Substance Abuse

Quoted in Katherine Ketcham and Nicholas A. Pace, *Teens Under the Influence: The Truth About Kids, Alcohol, and Other Drugs–How to Recognize the Problem and What to Do About It*. New York, NY: Ballantine, 2003, p. 75.

The risk of being involved in an accident is directly linked to how many miles people drive. "During the summer months, young drivers have more time on their hands and a care-free vacation attitude ... Combine this with the fact that they are inexperienced drivers and the number of crashes rises,"[38] said Martha Meade, manager of public and governmental relations for AAA Mid-Atlantic. The

Car crashes are a major cause of alcohol-related deaths for teens.

AAA Foundation for Traffic Safety's 2015 study found that car crashes for teens ages 16 to 17 were nearly double that of older teens. Statistics compiled by AAA show that from 2005 to 2009, more than 7,300 drivers and passengers ages 16 to 19 were killed in crashes between Memorial Day and Labor Day. Teen deaths during the summer averaged 442 per month, compared to an average of 363 teen deaths in non-summer months.

Alcohol is also a major factor in the increased number of auto accidents and fatalities teens have during the summer. Data from the U.S. National Highway Traffic Safety Administration (NHTSA) for 2015 showed that 1,908 teen drivers died in drunk driving crashes that year and that these drivers were less likely to be wearing their seat belts—58 percent of drunk teen drivers who died in a crash were unrestrained.

Legal Penalties

Even if no one is harmed when a teen drinks, someone under 21 who is caught drinking can face penalties simply for having alcohol in their possession. These vary from state to state and may depend on the age of the person who is drinking. Some possible penalties include:

- a fine of anywhere from $50 to $500
- community service hours
- a mandatory alcohol education class
- alcohol counseling, if the person shows signs of an alcohol use disorder
- a stay at a juvenile detention center, or in jail if the person is between the ages of 18 and 20
- suspension of the person's driver's license for up to one year, even if the person was not driving at the time (this applies across state lines)
- a charge of assault or resisting arrest if the person tries to fight the police while drunk

A Changing Brain

Scientists who study the brain have known for a long time that the brains of six-year-olds are 95 percent of the size they will be when the children are adults. In the past, scientists believed that because the brain was so large by then, it was mostly done developing and changing. More recent studies, however, have proven that the brain is still undergoing complex changes as late as a person's early 20s. Some of the most important changes happen in the frontal lobe, the part of the brain that helps people resist impulses and make good decisions.

Deborah Yurgelun-Todd, a psychiatry professor at the University of Utah, has studied how teenage brains influence teens' reactions to various situations. She believes the unfinished development of the frontal lobes of teenage brains makes it harder for teenagers to see the potential consequences of their behavior. Yurgelun-Todd claimed this incomplete development leads teenagers to act impulsively without properly assessing dangers involved in situations they encounter:

> *To appreciate what the consequences of a behavior are, you have to really think through what the potential outcomes of a behavior are. I think the frontal lobe ... is not always functioning fully in teenagers ...*
>
> *That would suggest that therefore teenagers aren't thinking through what the consequences of their behaviors are [and] they're not going to be so worried about whether or not what they're doing has a negative consequence.*[39]

One reason teens who drink and drive are more likely to be involved in accidents is that alcohol affects their brains differently than adults' brains. Alcohol is a depressant—people who drink enough alcohol eventually get sleepy and fall asleep or become unconscious. Alcohol, however, does not sedate teenage brains as much as it does those of adults. H. Scott Swartzwelder, a professor with the Duke University Institute for Brain Sciences, claimed this difference has a disastrous effect for teens who drink and drive: "If teenagers don't feel sleepy after they drink, they may think it's OK to get behind the wheel [of a car]."[40]

Due to the way their bodies process alcohol, most adults get very tired when they are drunk and tend to fall asleep. Teenagers have more natural energy and can stay awake longer while drunk. This gives them more time to make bad, alcohol-influenced decisions. At that point, one of alcohol's other effects on the teenage brain helps them make the dangerous decision to drive drunk. In *Teens Under the Influence*, Ketcham and Pace wrote that although alcohol does not sedate teenagers as strongly as it does adults, it has a more powerful effect on their sense of judgment:

> *While adolescents may be able to stay awake and keep drinking long after adult drinkers have tumbled into bed, their decision-making skills, judgment, and memory are more profoundly affected by the drug. They will think they can do things that they cannot do safely under the influence of [alcohol], and they may make decisions that put their lives or the lives of others at risk.*[41]

People make deadly mistakes when they assume that tragedy cannot happen to them. Sergeant Tim Bieber of the Clark County Sheriff's Office in the state of Washington has investigated numerous auto accidents involving alcohol. After several 2006 crashes involving intoxicated teenagers, Bieber said he believed so many teenagers risk driving after they have been drinking because of their mistaken belief that they will never be hurt or cause a serious accident: "A lot of it is this

A DEADLY RIDE

"Two nights before his death, I reminded my son not to drink, and not to get into a car with anyone who had been drinking. [He responded,] 'Trust me dad. I know better.'"

–Jeff Levy, discussing the death of his college-age son in 2009 when he was a passenger in a car driven by a drunk teenager who crashed

Quoted in Susan Larson, "Parents, Teens Discuss Perils of College Drinking Culture," *Burke Patch*, July 26, 2011. burke.patch.com/articles/parents-teens-discuss-perils-of-college-drinking-culture.

sense of invincibility [teens have]. Most kids that age don't think anything bad is going to happen."[42] That same feeling of invulnerability leads teenagers to ignore the need to fasten their seat belts, which increases their risk of injury or death.

Cars and Alcohol Do Not Mix

The reason the decision to drive is so destructive for anyone who has been drinking is that alcohol severely decreases their physical and mental ability to drive safely. People who are drunk have trouble talking, walking, and thinking because alcohol makes it difficult for their brains to direct their bodies to perform even simple tasks, such as walking in a straight line. The effect alcohol has on the way people drive is similar but even more dangerous. Instead of piloting only their body, a drunk driver is also controlling a vehicle that weighs several thousand pounds and can travel at speeds of more than 100 miles (161 km) per hour. Cars driven by drunk drivers become mobile missiles that can injure or kill the driver, passengers, or other people if they lose control.

Alcohol affects drivers in many ways: sight (vision becomes blurred and the driver has trouble seeing the road and other vehicles); motor skills (the ability to guide the car in a straight line, control speed, change lanes, or properly apply brakes); and the driver's mind (a weakened ability to understand what is happening to the car and to respond rapidly to changing road conditions such as oncoming vehicles or a traffic light turning red).

Driving is difficult after someone has been drinking because it slows their reaction time and makes it harder for them to see properly.

The higher a person's BAC, the more trouble they will have driving.

Although drinking and driving can have disastrous consequences, many teens are lucky enough to avoid them. This can give them and their friends a false sense of security; they may see it as proof that driving drunk does not have serious consequences, even though many others are involved in serious accidents. For example, Mike drove drunk many times when he was a teenager. He was never arrested for drunk driving and never had an accident, but he did back into a car once in a parking lot; he fled before anyone saw him because he was afraid of being arrested. Even though Mike never got into trouble, he admitted that driving drunk sometimes scared him:

> *It sometimes seemed like fun, it was kinda goofy. But it's hard to see, sometimes it looks like there are two or three cars coming at you when there's just one … Sometimes curves seemed to just be there when I thought the road was straight … that was bad. I even ran off [the road] a few times. And I was always worried about the cops.*[43]

Not everyone is so lucky when they drink and drive or get in a car with someone who has been drinking. On February 25, 2006, Jessica Rasdall and Laura Gorman, her best friend, went dancing at some clubs in Ybor City, Florida. Even though they were only 18 years old, they were served drinks and got drunk. Gorman died when Rasdall ran off Interstate 275 and smashed into a tree while driving her friend home after the bars closed at 3:00 a.m.

Rasdall was sentenced to four years in prison after she pleaded no contest to a charge of driving-under-the-influence manslaughter. However, Rasdall said she will continue to serve a lifetime sentence because of the emotional pain she will always feel over the death of Gorman: "I never blamed it on anybody else … I had a big court hearing. I got up and I said, 'I drank, I drove and I killed my best friend.'"[44]

Rasdall took responsibility for her actions and served her time in jail. Today, she is a motivational speaker who gives presentations at schools across the United States, speaking about the dangers of drunk driving as well as the need for people to face the consequences of their actions and take responsibility for their own lives. However, not all drunk drivers admit fault. In 2013, a teenager named Ethan Couch was arrested when he drove with a BAC of 0.24 percent and caused a crash that killed four people and injured two more. In court, he successfully avoided jail time when a psychologist argued that Couch had "affluenza," an invented word used to describe Couch as "a product of wealthy, privileged parents who never set limits for him."[45] He was sentenced to probation, but in 2015, he violated the terms of that probation when he and his mother fled to Mexico. They were found and returned to the United States, and Couch received two years of jail time for leaving the country and violating his probation. As of 2018, he still has not served any time for taking the lives of the people he killed. Mothers Against Drunk Driving (MADD) spoke of this as "a grave injustice to the victims and their families. The 720 days Ethan Couch served for his crimes shows that drunk driving homicides still aren't treated as the violent crimes that they are."[46]

Ethan Couch avoided punishment for killing four people in a drunken car crash by pleading that his "affluenza" made him unable to tell that what he was doing was wrong. He was later arrested for fleeing to Mexico.

SAME ALCOHOL, DIFFERENT RESPONSES

"Adolescents and adults respond in different ways to the same amount of alcohol. Compared to adults, adolescents tend to be less sensitive to alcohol's calming effect, and they are less sensitive to alcohol's effects on motor coordination. But when it comes to reasoning, logic, and memory–skills controlled by different brain structures–adolescents are much more vulnerable to alcohol-induced impairment."

–Katherine Ketcham and Nicholas A. Pace, authors of *Teens Under the Influence: The Truth About Kids, Alcohol, and Other Drugs–How to Recognize the Problem and What to Do About It*

Katherine Ketcham and Nicholas A. Pace, *Teens Under the Influence: The Truth About Kids, Alcohol, and Other Drugs–How to Recognize the Problem and What to Do About It*. New York, NY: Ballantine, 2003, p. 44.

Breaking the Law

Teenagers who want to drink have to obtain alcohol illegally. Sometimes it is as easy as finding a store that sells alcohol to teenagers. When Jack was in high school, he discovered a liquor store that would sell him beer, so he regularly went there and bought six-packs for his friends. He said he did it because "it made me a cool guy, a big time guy. That helped me be part of the group."[47] Many teens get older friends or siblings to buy alcohol for them, and some purchase it themselves with a fake ID. Teens also sometimes steal alcohol from their parents or the homes of people they know.

However teenagers get alcohol, they risk being punished just for being caught with it in their possession. For example, Greg began drinking when he was in seventh grade and continued even though he got into trouble several times. Greg once packed a bottle of vodka in his suitcase when he and some eighth-grade friends went to a cottage his parents owned during summer vacation. When his older sister found the bottle and told his father, his dad came up with an unusual punishment: "He made me and my friends go to mass every day at 7:15 a.m. under threat of telling everyone's parents if they did not show up. That was quite a way to spend the last two weeks of summer vacation."[48]

COLLEGE DRINKING CULTURE

"In high school, it needs to be hidden from parents. In the working world, it must be downplayed to bosses, or concerned friends, or lovers. But in college, we can wear our alcohol abuse as proudly as our university sweatshirt; the two concepts are virtually synonymous."

–Koren Zailckas, author of *Smashed: Story of a Drunken Girlhood*, on how young people accept heavy drinking as part of college life

Quoted in Anna Mundow, "The Lost Years of a 'Dead Drunk Daughter,'" *Irish Times*, February 23, 2005. www.irishtimes.com/newspaper/features/2005/0223/1107916262150.html

Perhaps the worst place to get caught with alcohol is school. Schools ban alcohol and other drugs, and school officials punish students who are caught with alcohol in school. In one extreme example, a large group of students showed up drunk at a prom at Methacton High School in Eagleville, Pennsylvania, in May 2011. Forty-one students were suspended from school for up to 10 days and were required to perform up to 20 hours of community service, such as cleaning graffiti from buildings. Student athletes who were part of the group were also suspended from their teams for 15 days.

Such punishments, however, seem minor compared to what can happen to teenagers who drink. All too often teens become seriously ill from drinking or die from alcohol poisoning.

Binge Drinking and Alcohol Poisoning

Teenagers, especially those who are not used to drinking, often do not understand how toxic large amounts of alcohol can be. Most medical emergencies involving alcohol occur

Know When to Get Help

When teens binge drink, they may go from laughing and talking one minute to vomiting and losing consciousness the next. It is important to know when to get help for people who choose to engage in binge drinking. Some signs of alcohol poisoning include:

- *Confusion*
- *Vomiting*
- *Seizures*
- *Slow breathing (less than eight breaths a minute)*
- *Irregular breathing (a gap of more than 10 seconds between breaths)*
- *Blue-tinged skin or pale skin*
- *Low body temperature (hypothermia)*
- *Passing out (unconsciousness) and can't be awakened*[1]

Someone with alcohol poisoning may not have all of these symptoms. It is important to get help if they seem unwell, especially if they have lost consciousness. Alcohol poisoning can easily lead to death, so getting help quickly is a priority, whether that means calling 911, telling a parent, or both. The person should never be left alone before help arrives. If someone who is unconscious is left lying on their back, they may die if they vomit; since they cannot wake up to roll over, they may choke on their vomit. They should be kept sitting up or lying with their head to the side to help prevent choking.

Some teens may be too worried about being punished for drinking to get help for a friend. Because alcohol poisoning endangers a person's life, some states or organizations–such as individual colleges–protect teens who call for help for a friend who has had too much to drink. These are known as Good Samaritan laws or medical amnesty policies, and the details vary from place to place.

1. Mayo Clinic Staff, "Alcohol Poisoning," Mayo Clinic, accessed on April 2, 2018, www.mayoclinic.org/diseases-conditions/alcohol-poisoning/symptoms-causes/syc-20354386.

during binge drinking sessions. In 2017, 90 teens were hospitalized due to severe intoxication at a concert in Hartford, Connecticut. According to John Brancato, the assistant director of a hospital's pediatric emergency department:

> *It's not like adult social drinking, where you're out with friends or family and you have a glass of wine or beer ... With the kids who get brought into the hospital, they drink with one sole purpose [to get as drunk as possible], and they don't understand anything about how their bodies will handle it.*[49]

The CDC has reported that there are more than 2,200 alcohol poisoning deaths each year, which is an average of 6 alcohol poisoning deaths every day. People between the ages of 15 and 24 make up about 5 percent of these deaths. College students, in particular, are known for drinking more alcohol than the average person.

The NIAAA estimates that at least 1,800 college students die annually from alcohol-related causes—including car crashes, falls, burns, and drowning—and many more are injured by these accidents. The NIAAA believes heavy drinking among college students, most of them younger than 21, is due to a culture of alcohol use that has developed over many years:

> *Customs that promote college drinking ... are embedded in numerous levels of students' environments ...*
>
> *Environmental and peer influences combine to create a culture of drinking. This culture actively promotes drinking, or passively promotes it, through tolerance, or even tacit approval, of college drinking as a rite of passage.*[50]

More than 37 percent of college students engage in binge drinking, compared with about 32.6 percent of non-college students of the same age. Binge drinking among college students often includes drinking games, which can distract someone from keeping track of how much they have had to drink. Games that are fast-paced are especially dangerous, as they can cause someone to drink a lot before the effects

Fast-paced drinking games such as beer pong make it easy for someone to get drunk before they even realize it is happening.

start becoming apparent. By the time they start feeling different, they may have already drunk too much without realizing it.

Peer pressure often plays its role in this drinking culture. It is not uncommon for college students to encourage their friends to drink more, no matter how much they have already had to drink. As a night of drinking goes on, everyone's judgment becomes impaired, and someone may encourage a friend to drink—while being too drunk themselves to see that this could become dangerous. Putting pressure on someone to drink is often not done with bad intentions; someone may truly believe their friend would have more fun if they were drinking, or they may feel insecure about their own drinking. According to the website The Conversation, "if we tend to associate with people who are like us and engage in similar behaviors, and we start doing things in a way that goes against the group norms, such as not drinking in a social situation, this can be a challenge to the acceptability of that behaviour in the group."[51]

Some people may feel as though they need to drink when their friends tell them to, as a way to prove they can keep up with the group. However, it is important to remember that good friends will not keep pressuring someone into doing something they feel uncomfortable with. If someone has stated that they feel uncomfortable drinking and the people around them keep trying to give them alcohol in spite of this statement, it is a sign that the non-drinker should remove themselves from the situation.

Another dangerous thing teens sometimes do is mix alcohol with other drugs, including prescription drugs, which are often stolen from home. Sometimes this happens accidentally—for instance, if someone is taking a prescription medication and is unaware that it has negative side effects when mixed with alcohol. Many times, however, people choose to combine drugs and alcohol "because they mistakenly believe it will be a 'better' or 'enriched' intoxication."[52]

Nora Volkow, director of the National Institute on Drug Abuse (NIDA), warned that mixing alcohol with OxyContin, Vicodin, Xanax, Valium, ecstasy, and other drugs is extremely dangerous. Volkow noted that teenagers do not know how a mixture of drugs and alcohol will affect them. Even if they have taken them together before, the effects often vary. Combining alcohol and other drugs can result in serious sickness, hospitalization, and death, especially if someone takes even a little too much—and it is difficult to know how much is too much until that threshold has been passed. Many people have died this way. Someone who makes a mistake by mixing drugs and alcohol often does not get a second chance.

DRINKING CAN KILL ANYWHERE

"I think society has taught kids so well to not drink and drive. But they don't realize that it can be dangerous to drink and stay at home."

–Angie Ammon, after her 19-year-old daughter, Molly, died of alcohol poisoning

Quoted in Jessica Vander Velde, "UF Freshman from Tampa Found Dead by Friends in Madeira Beach Condo," *St. Petersburg Times*, March 15, 2011. www.tampabay.com/news/publicsafety/uf-freshman-from-tampa-found-dead-by-friends-in-madeira-beach-condo/1157270a.

Even mixing "safe" drugs with alcohol can have disastrous effects. Acetaminophen (Tylenol) is an over-the-counter

Mixing drugs and alcohol often has very dangerous outcomes. Even drugs that are legal can be deadly when mixed with alcohol.

pain medication commonly used to treat mild headaches and fever. Someone who frequently takes acetaminophen while drinking heavily can develop acute liver damage, which happens much more quickly than cirrhosis. Symptoms of acute liver damage can develop within hours, and irreversible damage can be done in just a few days. These symptoms, which are often severe, include abdominal pain and swelling, loss of appetite, vomiting, sweating, confusion, and abnormal bruising or bleeding. While some people recover after a few weeks, others die from this condition.

Young women and trans men who are biologically female face more dangers than their male counterparts when they drink heavily. Mark Willenbring, a doctor with the NIAAA, said females should be even more careful than males when they drink because they generally weigh less and their bodies absorb alcohol differently than men's bodies. Both factors mean that if a female drinks the same amount of alcohol as a male, she will likely become drunk more quickly. Females are also more likely to black out. "In a blackout, you're still conscious—you're walking, and talking, and interacting with people, but later you won't remember anything, because long-term memory storage has been disabled," wrote Sarah Hepola, author of *Blackout: Remembering the Things I Drank to Forget*. "It's basically a temporary amnesia brought on by drinking too much—especially drinking fast, and on an empty stomach."[53] Willenbring said women are especially at risk if they participate in drinking games that force them to quickly drink a lot of alcohol.

DENIAL ABOUT DRINKING TOO MUCH

"I was 21 and drinking was still, mostly, fun. I was getting great grades. But there were warning signs; people I wouldn't hang out with because they were boring (didn't drink more than a glass or two on weeknights) and classes I missed because I was too hungover to make it in. I had to borrow money to pay rent and bills, because I was spending my earnings and savings on booze and drugs. Time passed and I dropped out of university because, I told myself, 'I don't want this.' Actually, I was failing that semester because I was drinking and drugging so heavily that I couldn't do course work or pass exams."

–Karen Opas, editor, on developing an alcohol use disorder without realizing it

Karen Opas, "What It's Like to Be an Alcoholic," *Business Insider*, February 13, 2014. www.businessinsider.com/heres-what-its-like-to-be-an-alcoholic-2014-2

The Risk of Sexual Assault

Sexual assault is another risk people face when drinking. Both men and women can be targets, although in most cases, men are the aggressors and women are the targets. It is estimated that 97,000 college students each year are victims of alcohol-related sexual assault or date rape. The Rape, Abuse and Incest National Network (RAINN) states that 1 in 6 women will be victims of sexual assault during their lifetime and that girls ages 16 to 19 are 4 times more likely than women in any other age group to be victims of rape, attempted rape, or sexual assault. Alcohol is a common factor in sexual assault

A drunk person who is alone is more likely to be targeted by a rapist. Staying close to friends who have had too much to drink is one way to minimize this risk.

because men are more likely to assault someone if they believe their victim is too drunk to fight back.

In January 2015, alcohol led to the sexual assault of a 23-year-old woman by 19-year-old Brock Turner on an American college campus. Two Swedish students passing by a dumpster on campus saw Turner assaulting the unconscious woman and intervened to stop the assault.

The victim described Turner as a predator picking off "the wounded antelope of the herd, completely alone and vulnerable, physically unable to fend for myself."[54] Like Ethan Couch, Turner tried to use an argument about the culture around him to show that he was not responsible for his own actions: He blamed the drinking culture of college for encouraging him to drink. However, one meta-study (study of many previous studies) of sexual assault found that men "who commit sexual assault when drinking alcohol are similar to men who commit sexual assault when sober in most aspects of their personality and attitudes."[55] The court believed that alcohol was not an excuse and that Turner, like other sex offenders, knew that what he was doing was wrong. He was convicted of sexual assault, lost his scholarship and place on the swim team, and is now a registered sex offender. The prosecutors in the case wanted a six-year prison sentence, but he only received six months in jail because the judge worried about the impact on Turner's future.

Deborah Gardner, a spokesperson for the Women's Center of Tarrant County, Texas, said when a woman is intoxicated, she cannot give permission to someone to have sex with her. She also stressed that even though women are often blamed when they are raped after they have been drinking, such incidents are not the victim's fault: "People make mistakes all the time, and we put ourselves in vulnerable situations all the time. But it doesn't justify someone else's faulty thinking or their deviancy."[56] As the *Washington Post* pointed out, "Alcohol may be used as a weapon, or an excuse for aggressive behavior. But the only thing necessary for a rape to happen is the presence of a rapist."[57]

Taking Responsibility

It is a fact of life that everyone makes mistakes, even good people. However, it is important for people to own up to those mistakes, apologize, and do what they can to make it right, the way Jessica Rasdall did. When people such as Couch and Turner try to avoid consequences by pointing out that they are generally good people, they miss an important point–one that was summarized by Joseph, an online commentator reacting to a news story about a drunk driving crash. He wrote, "We have a situation where two people died because of someone's selfish decision to drive while intoxicated. Regardless of whether [the driver] is a 'good' or 'bad' person isn't the issue here. The real issue is drunk driving [and] how much damage it does to families."[1]

In an article for the *Washington Post*, a woman named Kate Geiselman who lived in Turner's community wrote that many of the teens raised in that town were never punished by their parents for things they did wrong. Many people supported him after his trial, blaming alcohol for his actions and talking about how he was otherwise a good person. Geiselman wrote about the way she wished Turner had acted instead and how people's personal interactions with him did not erase his violent actions:

Although it is never the victim's fault for drinking, it is wise for drinkers to be aware of the risks around them. People who are drinking can take several basic precautions to give themselves some peace of mind and a feeling of control, such as pouring their own drinks or watching them be poured so they can tell how much alcohol is in them; counting their drinks so they know when they have reached their limit; and going to parties with at least one friend they trust. Many people are concerned about the possibility of drugs being slipped into a person's drink, but studies indicate that

He looks his victim squarely in the eyes and says: "I'm sorry … I will do everything I can to spare you any further pain. I will spend the rest of my life educating young people about consent and sexual violence."

Then he serves his punishment, perhaps a sentence mitigated [lessened] by his understanding of the crime, his taking responsibility, even his character references—because he gets it. He bears the weight of his guilt and in doing so eases the burden of his victim …

No, I don't "know" Turner like his friends or neighbors do. But I do know what he did, and so do we all, based on the unanimous verdict of a jury and testimony from two witnesses. We now also know exactly what his victim suffered, and we know that he doesn't own [take responsibility for] any of it. Neither do his apologists.[2]

Alcohol is never an excuse for someone's bad behavior. If someone cannot trust themselves to make good decisions after they have been drinking, they should not drink at all, even if they are an adult. Any mistakes they make or crimes they commit while drunk should be acknowledged, and they need to take responsibility for those actions.

1. Joseph, comment on Craig Day, "Claremore Teen Arrested After Suspected DUI Crash Kills Man, Baby," KOTV.com, June 17, 2011. www.newsone.com/story/14927478/two-killed-in-friday-morning-crash-on-66-in-verdigris.

2. Kate Geiselman, "In Brock Turner's Home Town, We're Raising Kids Who Are Never Told 'No,'" *Washington Post*, June 8, 2016. www.washingtonpost.com/posteverything/wp/2016/06/08/in-brock-turners-hometown-were-raising-kids-who-are-never-told-no/?utm_term=.1a2a1e0bfa9d.

the most common way for a rapist to incapacitate their victim is to give them more alcohol than they were aware they were drinking so they get more drunk than they were expecting to. However, some rapists do give their victims other types of drugs, and it is easy for them to slip a pill into a drink when the drinker is not paying attention. To minimize this risk, a person should keep their drink close and not drink from a cup or glass again if they have to set it down for any reason.

The *Washington Post* noted that when people are willing to speak up and stop behavior they know is wrong, such as the way the two Swedish students stopped Turner, rapists have less opportunity to assault someone. However, the *Washington Post* also cautioned,

> *Bystander intervention isn't going to end sexual violence alone, obviously. We need to educate boys and men about healthy masculinity, and equip women and girls with skills to set boundaries and protect themselves from attacks. But we can all work to create a culture where violence isn't tolerated and where everyone plays a role in making our communities safer.*[58]

Addiction in the Teenage Brain

Because teenage brains are still developing, alcohol affects them differently than it does adult brains. Aaron White, senior scientific advisor to the director of the NIAAA, has written studies about the effects of heavy drinking by college students. He said, "There is no doubt about it now: there are long-term cognitive consequences to excessive drinking of alcohol in adolescence."[59]

One study showed that teens who had consumed at least two drinks a day for two years were able to remember 10 percent less on memory tests than nondrinking teenagers. That memory weakness was large enough to make it harder for students to pass tests requiring memorization. Such damage to the way the brain operates, however, is not the only way alcohol hurts teenage brains.

Evidence shows that people who start drinking in their teens have a far greater chance of developing an alcohol use disorder.

Warning Signs of an Alcohol Use Disorder

An alcohol use disorder can range from mild to severe, but at any level, it is a problem. While some people with this disorder end up in financial or legal trouble, lose their jobs because of drinking at work or coming in hungover, or end up doing nothing but drinking all day, others are considered functional, or high-functioning, alcoholics. These people may reassure themselves that they do not have to worry about having an alcohol use disorder because they have not hit rock-bottom, but they are still letting alcohol control their lives and likely suffering unknown health problems. Some of the warning signs of an alcohol use disorder include:

- drinking in secret or at odd times of day, such as first thing in the morning
- hiding alcohol to make sure it is always available (for instance, hiding a bottle in the bathroom at school)
- needing alcohol to feel relaxed or sociable
- letting responsibilities slip—for example, missing classes or not doing homework
- frequently getting drunk unintentionally
- frequently forgetting what happened while drunk
- engaging in risky behavior, such as driving drunk or having unprotected sex with strangers
- wanting to stop drinking but feeling unable to
- losing friendships or getting angry when someone expresses concern about the amount the person is drinking
- always being aware of when they can have their next drink and feeling distressed if they do not have access to alcohol

According to the fifth edition of the *Diagnostic and Statistical Manual of Mental Disorders (DSM-5)*, this is the new preferred term for what was previously called alcoholism. However, most people are unaware of this new term and continue to call it alcoholism. Both terms mean the same thing: an addiction to alcohol.

The Surgeon General of the United States defines someone with alcohol dependence as a person who has "trouble controlling their drinking, and when their consumption of, or preoccupation with, alcohol occurs to the extent that it interferes with normal personal, family, social, or work life."[60]

Multiple studies over the years have shown that drinking in the teenage years can increase this risk. A 2006 study showed that 47 percent of people who began drinking alcohol before age 14 became alcohol dependent at some time in their lives; that figure was compared with the 9 percent of people who did not drink until they were 21.

As of 2017, about 12.7 percent of American adults met the criteria for an alcohol use disorder. The 2015 National Survey on Drug Use and Health (NSDUH) estimated that more than 600,000 teenagers were problem drinkers, identified in the study as a person who has an alcohol use disorder.

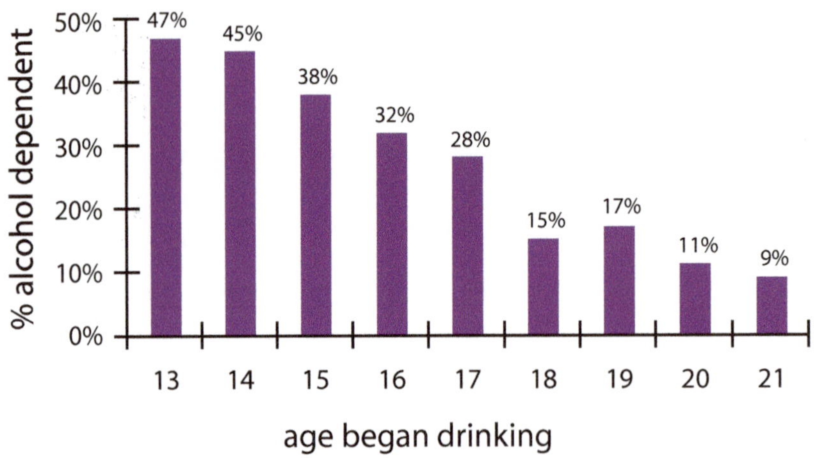

The younger a person starts drinking, the greater the chance that they will develop an alcohol use disorder, according to the National Epidemiologic Survey on Alcohol and Related Conditions.

People with an alcohol use disorder are generally unable to quit drinking without professional help. Although at first they drink because they enjoy how it makes them feel, eventually they get to the point where they do not feel as though they can function when sober. For this reason, they will keep drinking even when they and the people around them start suffering consequences. They use alcohol as a coping mechanism to help them deal with unpleasant feelings, so as their lives start to become more unpleasant as a result of their drinking—losing a job, encountering financial problems from buying so much alcohol, having disagreements with family members about their drinking—they turn back to alcohol to help them, which only makes the problem worse. Karen Opas, who struggled with an alcohol use disorder throughout her youth, wrote,

> *Drinking pretty much took over my life. I had a few friends who drank as hard as I did. We prided ourselves on it and thought the rest of the world were boring sheep with no sense of adventure. I did things I was ashamed of … [such as] stealing from friends and convincing myself it wasn't theft, that they owed me or would want me to have it. I was best woman at a childhood friend's wedding and I didn't show up for the ceremony. I had gotten drunk the night before and, truthfully, didn't want to stand up and watch someone be happy and move forward in life.*[61]

Eventually Opas beat her addiction and moved on to live a happy, fulfilling life. However, it took years of denial, heavy drinking, and at least one near-death experience for her to get to that point. Teens who choose not to drink decrease their risk of having to battle addiction later in life.

Choosing Wisely: Prevention

Preventing alcohol use and abuse by teens is a community job. One group called Voices of Youth in Chicago Education (VOYCE) studied underage drinking. The group found that youth in Chicago were often using alcohol due to a number of factors, such as mental health problems, trauma caused by Chicago's high rate of violence, and school stress. Another factor in underage drinking is the normalization of alcohol. Teens look around and see alcohol depicted as fun by advertisements, movies, and even their parents. When teens drink, their peers tend to look the other way; they often know what is happening but do not want to be seen as someone who would betray a secret. In reality, telling someone is often the first step toward getting help. "Youssef had brought alcohol to school and drank it in the bathroom, and everyone knew he was drinking," eighth-grader Jovianne Ojeda Degillo confessed about her classmate. "Everyone knew about this, but didn't mention it to anyone that could help and the issues were never addressed."[62]

The effort to curb teenage drinking and safeguard young people against the dangers of using alcohol requires the effort of everyone in the community. That fight against underage drinking is being waged across the nation by government agencies, private groups, and teens themselves.

Using Scare Tactics

Since underage drinking is both a legal and a public health issue, it is a concern for federal, state, and local government agencies, especially in places where teens and college students gather for spring break. "There is zero tolerance for criminal behavior," said Sheriff Tommy Ford of Panama City Beach in Florida. "Use common sense and leave Spring Break with a great suntan, not a criminal record."[63]

Private organizations such as Mothers Against Drunk Driving (MADD) and Students Against Destructive Decisions (SADD) also fight underage drinking. Most of their efforts are aimed at educating teenagers and the general public about the many effects of alcohol. Government agencies, individuals, and groups involved in this fight use a wide variety of methods to accomplish that goal.

SADD helps educate teens through school assemblies and sometimes a staged "death" of a student and the display of a smashed car. On March 25, 2011, the day before the prom at Alexandria High School in Alexandria, Alabama, Calhoun County deputies staged a mock fatal accident at the school, complete with a smashed-up car, empty beer cans, and two victims who were taken away by an ambulance. The event was organized by the school's SADD affiliate to show students what can happen if they drink and drive. Sophomore Carly Edwards said the dramatization was an eye-opener for her: "It's scary. I'm sure this will send a message to some people who don't think about the consequences."[64] However, these scare tactics can be very traumatic and are not proven to provide long-term deterrence; in fact, some studies have shown that scare tactics may increase the likelihood that a teen will engage in dangerous behavior.

A Community Approach to the Problem

Other countries take a different approach to ending underage drinking. Iceland used to have the heaviest-drinking teenagers in all of Europe. "You couldn't walk the streets in downtown Reykjavik on a Friday night because it felt unsafe," said Harvey Milkman, an American psychology professor who conducted research into American teens' drug and alcohol use in the 1990s. Milkman said, "There were hordes of teenagers getting in-your-face drunk."[65] Due to a program called Youth in Iceland, though, the drinking rate has plummeted. From 1998 to 2016, the percent of teens ages 15 and 16 who had been drunk in the previous month decreased from 42 percent to 5 percent. Other types of drug abuse also plummeted: Cannabis use decreased from

17 percent to 7 percent, and daily cigarette smoking decreased from 23 percent to 3 percent.

Milkman's research was instrumental in the turnaround. He and his team of researchers in the United States discovered that drug and alcohol abuse in teens was often driven by behavioral factors. Using his research, an Icelandic researcher named Inga Dóra Sigfúsdóttir conducted her own research to help Iceland develop Youth in Iceland, a program that helps teens rely on their own body chemistry to feel good again. In Iceland, that means the city governments invested in sports, the arts, music, and giving kids and their parents time together. Every family receives money to spend on kids' programs and is encouraged to participate in the local schools.

The program Youth in Iceland dramatically reduced teens' rates of drug and alcohol use, especially in the city of Reykjavik (shown here).

Youth in Iceland helped change a lot of rules for everyone in Iceland. Alcohol and tobacco ads were banned. A curfew of 10:00 p.m. was set for teens, and parents pledged not to provide alcohol or have unsupervised parties in their homes. Parents were also asked to pledge to watch out for each other's children by taking walks around their neighborhood to catch rule breakers. By creating a feeling of community, parents all over Reykjavik began to

ENJOYING LIFE INSTEAD OF ALCOHOL

"We learned through the studies that we need to create circumstances in which kids can lead healthy lives, and they do not need to use substances, because life is fun, and they have plenty to do—and they are supported by parents who will spend time with them."

—Inga Dóra Sigfúsdóttir, researcher

Quoted in Emma Young, "How Iceland Got Teens to Say No to Drugs," *The Atlantic*, January 19, 2017. www.theatlantic.com/health/archive/2017/01/teens-drugs-iceland/513668/

be accountable for every teen, and the results were so dramatic that other European cities wanted to adopt the same strategies. In 2006, a program called Youth in Europe was created, and as of 2017, 35 cities across 17 countries have taken part in it.

In the United States, where this type of program does not exist, some individuals have tried various strategies to make teens aware of the dangers of underage drinking. For instance, Imbler High School senior Kiley Dewey won a statewide award in Oregon for fighting drunk driving for the one-day Living Dead program she organized at her school on October 20, 2008. In the United States, a teenager dies on average every 15 minutes in a drunk driving crash. Over a 3-hour period, an Imbler High School student was chosen every 15 minutes to become a victim. They were wheeled out of class on a gurney, then they put on white makeup and hooded cloaks. When they went to classes in costume, they reminded other students about how many teens die in such accidents.

For many young people, drinking either starts or escalates when they go to college. When drinking at off-campus housing at the University of Wisconsin–Platteville became a problem because of loud parties and vandalism by drunk students, the SAFE (Safe Actions for Everyone) Grant County Coalition decided to act. In 2010, it started the Fresh Start program, which educated students about their out-of-control behavior instead of punishing them. Fresh Start allowed students to avoid being ticketed or fined for underage drinking by taking a course that taught them about the

NOT MAKING THE CONNECTION

"People think, 'It's not going to happen to me' or 'I'll never drink that much again.' They do not seem to associate their own heavy drinking with negative consequences."

–Kevin King, coauthor of a study on why some college students continue to drink despite problems associated with their alcohol use

Quoted in Molly McElroy, "Rose-Colored Beer Goggles: Social Benefits of Heavy Drinking Outweigh Harms," *UW Today*, July 5, 2011. www.washington.edu/news/articles/rose-colored-beer-goggles-social-benefits-of-heavy-drinking-outweigh-harms

Percentage of Teens in High School, Aged 16 Years or Older, Who Reported Drinking and Driving, by State

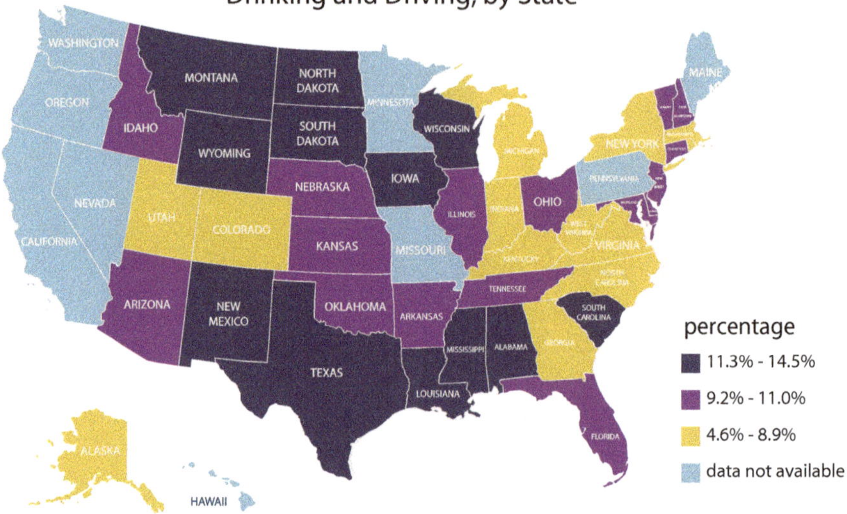

Teens in some states are more likely to drive drunk than in others, as this information from the CDC shows.

dangers associated with underage drinking. Kathy A. Marty, the group's director, said, "We want to educate, too, not just penalize [punish]."[66] The group encouraged students to host nonalcoholic parties by awarding a cash prize to the best party each year.

Some programs make a point to engage young adults. This is because "evidence shows that a peer-to-peer message is far more powerful than someone speaking at someone else … When young people send the message not to drink, it's very powerful."[67] One such program is the Meriden Healthy Youth Coalition in Meriden, Connecticut, where young adults are doing things such as putting stickers on a local liquor store's bags. The stickers have statistics on them that educate people about how widespread the problem of teen drinking is and asks adults not to provide alcohol to young people. Eighteen-year-old Mitchell McEwen, a member of the coalition, said the experience has been positive: "We feel like we're actually making a change in the world … Once I joined [the coalition,] I realized how much it can teach myself and the peers around me what alcohol and drugs can do to you."[68] The owner of the liquor store agreed, saying he has had a positive reaction from his customers when they see the stickers.

Although general education and innovative programs have helped curb teenage drinking, they have failed to stop it entirely. Teens who do drink, as well as adults who provide them with alcohol, risk being arrested and put in jail because of strict enforcement of underage drinking laws.

Breaking the Law for a Buzz

Few teenagers who drink ever stop to think that they could be arrested for doing so. However, it happens every day to hundreds of teens. In Taunton, Massachusetts, illegal IDs became such a big problem during the summer of 2011 that police began a crackdown on them. The town won a $9,700 grant to increase its surveillance of underage drinking, including undercover operations to find outlets that sold alcohol to teens using fake IDs. Police Sergeant Kevin Medas warned that teens caught with liquor would be fined and arrested on misdemeanor charges of illegal possession.

Teenagers often have parties at home because police in many states are not allowed to enter a private home unless they have knowledge that a crime is being committed. In the last few decades, however, communities have begun passing laws to make it easier for police to arrest teens at such parties. On August 22, 2011, Bay Head, New Jersey, officials adopted an ordinance that gave police greater power to enter homes and break up underage parties. Bay Head mayor William W. Curtis explained why his city needed a stronger law to police teen drinking: "What concerns me the most is that it seems the drinkers are younger now … We used to get high school–age kids having the parties, but now we've had kids as young as 13 having drinking parties."[69]

Not all such parties are unsupervised. Some parents believe that by hosting parties for their children and providing alcohol, they are making drinking safer and allowing teens to avoid potentially getting arrested while trying to obtain alcohol. Some parents also do it because they believe it makes their children and children's friends see them as "cool" parents. This was made fun of in the 2004 movie *Mean Girls*: When the main character, Cady, asks her friend's mother if the drink she has given Cady has alcohol in it, the mother responds, "Oh, God, honey, no! What kind of mother

Many teens who drink do so in someone's house because they believe it will minimize their risk of being caught. However, such parties often get out of hand, and the noise may lead neighbors to call the police.

do you think I am? Why, do you want a little bit? 'Cause if you're gonna drink, I'd rather you do it in the house."[70] She then goes on to try to gossip with the girls, showing that her offer of alcohol was an attempt to be one of the group rather than an authority figure.

The hosts of such parties are committing crimes by providing alcohol to minors and are mistaken in the belief that teens are safer if they drink in a parent's house. For this reason, a social hosting law was passed in Barrington, Illinois, that allows the city to fine parents who host parties for underage drinkers. Barrington was one of many Illinois communities that passed such laws after the 2006 deaths of two 18-year-olds. The teens were killed in a car crash after they had been drinking at a party in Deerfield, Illinois, that parents had held for their son and his friends.

In Bethesda, Maryland, high school principal Alan Goodwin sent an email out to community parents in November 2015, begging them to stop hosting parties for their teens. This was prompted by the knowledge that parents are ignoring the issues they see around them:

> *Three kids dead in Montgomery County in a little more than a year, thousands of pledges signed by parents promising not to serve alcohol to kids, a former high school quarterback indicted this week in the drunken-driving deaths of his two friends, a dad facing fines for allegedly hosting the party where they got drunk. Yet still, Goodwin heard that not just one, but two parents hosted drinking parties over Halloween weekend …*

It's not just the driving you have to worry about, Goodwin said. Sexual assault, alcohol poisoning. Someone falls off a deck.[71]

MODEL GOOD BEHAVIOR

"To reduce the risk of alcohol-related harm, parents should avoid supplying alcohol to children ... Modeling responsible alcohol consumption, enforcing strict alcohol related rules and monitoring of child behavior may also minimize risks of children using or misusing alcohol."

–Richard Mattick, lead researcher from the National Drug and Alcohol Research Center at the University of New South Wales in Sydney, Australia

Quoted in Lisa Rapaport, "Letting Teens Imbibe a Little to Teach Responsible Drinking Seems to Backfire, Study Finds," *Washington Post*, February 19, 2018. www.washingtonpost.com/national/health-science/letting-teens-imbibe-a-little-to-teach-responsible-drinking-seems-to-backfire-study-finds/2018/02/16/95190c12-126c-11e8-9570-29c9830535e5_story.html?utm_term=.79da58ad9614

Teens who believe they are being safe when they drink at a party hosted by an adult they know are not looking at the full picture of what can happen in these situations and are ignoring the long-term health risks they take when they drink at any time.

One way states have fought teenage drinking is to pass zero-tolerance laws, which make it illegal for anyone under 21 to drive with any amount of alcohol in their body. In some states, the limit is as low as 0.01 percent. The law that raised the drinking age to 21 specifies that a person must be caught with alcohol in their possession in order to be arrested, so someone who had this small amount of alcohol in their system with no alcohol in sight—for

BAC is often estimated using a Breathalyzer test, which is shown here.

Communication Is Key

Teens who feel like they can communicate with their parents or guardians about drinking often have a healthier relationship with alcohol. Parents or guardians who make it clear that they expect their teen to wait until age 21 to drink can help young adults avoid alcohol. However, sometimes teens give in to peer pressure, and knowing they can have an open conversation with a parent or guardian is an important way to stay on the right track.

Starting a conversation about drinking is hard, but it is also important. Listening is key: Parents or guardians need to listen to teens when they speak honestly about how peer pressure makes them feel, their desire to try alcohol, and the experiences they may have already had with underage drinking. In turn, teens need to listen to what their parents or guardians have to say about drinking even if they do not like it. Most likely, the adults want to be helpful, but they may not know exactly what to say; teens should not assume everything they say is meant to annoy them.

Being honest and demonstrating trustworthy behavior in other areas of their life may make a teen's guardians

instance, if they were walking home from a party—would generally not be arrested for underage drinking. A zero-tolerance DUI policy allows police to suspend an underage drunk driver's license without changing the original law. Having this type of crime on their record can affect their college acceptance prospects as well. This has made many teens think twice about driving after they have been drinking. In 2005, Jeanne Mejeur of the National Conference of State Legislatures wrote that the laws were a factor in a 6 percent decline nationwide from 1993 to 2003 in incidents involving teen drivers who had been drinking. However, Mejeur noted that "despite the improvement, far too many young drivers are still hitting the road after hitting the bottle. Reducing their access to alcohol is critical in saving lives."[72]

or parents be lenient about punishment for underage drinking. According to a North Carolina program called Absolute Advocacy, "Your parents will start to respect your opinion and trust you more if you are open about your experience with alcohol. They may be disappointed if you tried it illegally, but by being upfront with them it tells them that you are responsible enough to come clean."[1]

Open communication between teens and their parents or guardians is essential. Teens who feel able to discuss drinking with the adults in their life have a much healthier relationship with alcohol.

1. Keisha McLean-Green, "How to Talk to Your Parents About Alcohol," Absolute Advocacy, January 5, 2016. www.absoluteadvocacy.org/how-to-talk-to-your-parents-about-alcohol/

The harsh reality of teenage drinking is that some teenagers will drink despite the best efforts of government agencies, private groups, and individuals trying to make them realize how dangerous drinking can be for them. There are several factors that account for continued teenage drinking even though it is illegal and unsafe.

Drinking Still Appeals

The 1986 book *A Six-Pack and a Fake I.D.* by Susan and Daniel Cohen is a serious look at the many problems drinking creates for teenagers. In the book, the husband-and-wife writing team admitted honestly that they had been underage drinkers: "We both drank as teenagers, even though it was illegal to do so just as most other teenagers did then and do now. In school we were shown anti-drinking films [and] we laughed at them and ignored their message."[73]

Like the Cohens, many teenagers laugh off warnings about drinking from parents, teachers, the news media, and even other young adults. The fact that so many teens reject such advice and set aside factual evidence about the dangers drinking poses to them is frustrating to those who are trying to reduce underage drinking. The main reason young people ignore warnings about alcohol is that most have not experienced any of the serious negative consequences of drinking, such as killing someone in a car accident or developing an alcohol use disorder.

CREATING A MORE SERIOUS PROBLEM

"We want to forgive and overlook youthful indiscretions. [But by] not punishing the kids earlier, it becomes more serious as an adult problem."

–W. Clay Abbott of the Texas District and County Attorneys Association, explaining why Texas should be harder on teens who drink and drive

Quoted in Diane Jennings, Selwyn Crawford, and Dariean Spangenberger, "As Teens Drink and Drive, Texas Only Talks Tough," *Dallas Morning News*, January 2, 2011. www.dallas-news.com/news/crime/headlines/20110102-as-teens-drink-and-drive-texas-only-talks-tough-.ece.

On May 30, 2011, University of Washington (UW) psychologists released a study on why college students continue to drink even after they have experienced negative results such as hangovers, fights, and sexual contact they later realized was inappropriate or even dangerous. Their research included online responses from nearly 500 students who discussed their drinking. Diane Logan, a UW clinical psychology graduate student, said the study showed that students who had only minor problems from drinking kept using alcohol because they believed the benefits outweighed the risk that something worse might happen. Logan wrote, "Until high levels of negative consequences are

Never Too Young to Stop

One of the most effective ways for people with an alcohol use disorder to quit drinking is to go to meetings of Alcoholics Anonymous (AA). Even though most AA members are adults, teenagers are welcome at meetings. There are even meetings held just for teenagers called Young People in Alcoholics Anonymous (YPAA).

At 17, a young woman named Regan had a serious problem with alcohol. After fights with her family, dropping grades, and trying to run away, Regan knew she needed to do something different. "I couldn't continue living the way I was. I was going to die,"[1] she recalled in an interview. With the help of a treatment center that led her to AA, Regan was able to get sober. Being around people her own age was instrumental in her sobriety: "Young people in recovery care for each other ... They need each other. They need to see that other people can do it so they can do it."[2]

1. Quoted in Kate Parrish, "How This Teen Beat Alcoholism at 17," *Teen Vogue*, February 16, 2016. www.teenvogue.com/story/teen-alcoholism.
2. Quoted in Parrish, "How This Teen Beat Alcoholism at 17."

experienced, participants aren't deterred by the ill effects of drinking."[74] The same pattern of ignoring negative consequences that come from drinking can also lead adults to continue drinking despite health and social problems alcohol may cause them. Fortunately, though, fewer teens are drinking now than in the past.

The Age of Experience: 18 or 21?

In the past, the drinking age in the United States was 18. This was raised to 21 due to concerns about drinking and driving. However, many people in recent years have protested this for a variety of reasons. Some people who believe the drinking age should be lowered argue that 21 is an arbitrary, or random, age to allow people to consume alcohol. In the past, Americans were considered adults when they turned 21 because it was the age at which they could vote, but this reasoning is no longer valid because the current voting age is 18. Also, the drinking age is below 21 in almost every other country in the world; only 6 countries besides the United States set the minimum drinking age at 21.

Cynthia Garcia Coll, associate director of the Institutional Center of Scientific Research at Albizu University at San Juan, Puerto Rico, grew up in Puerto Rico. The drinking age there is 18, and Coll said Puerto Ricans allowed teenagers to drink at family parties to teach them how to drink safely. She claimed it is foolish to prohibit older teens from drinking and then, in an instant, allow them to consume as much alcohol as they want just because they turn 21: "In [the United States], we go from saying "No, you can't do it,' and then all at once, we say 'Yes, you can' without really giving them any guidance. It's not like age 21 is a magic time when people become responsible drinkers."[75]

John McCardell is the founder of Choose Responsibility, a group that wants to lower the drinking age. McCardell, the former president of Middlebury College in Vermont, believes the higher age creates dangerous drinking patterns for young

The ancient Greeks believed wearing an amethyst or drinking alcohol from an amethyst cup would prevent someone from getting drunk. It is from this myth that the Amethyst Initiative took its name.

people ages 18 to 20: "It's bad social policy and bad law. Prohibition does not work. Those [under 21] who are choosing to drink are drinking much more recklessly, and it's gone behind closed doors and underground and off-campus."[76] The group, however, recommends that a lower drinking age would also be bad policy unless it is coupled with increased education about alcohol—teens would have to pass a course on drinking to gain that privilege—and strict regulation of teens who do drink.

McCardell developed this view by witnessing binge drinking on college campuses. Because teens cannot drink legally, some say that they drink more heavily when they have the opportunity. The results of binge drinking can be disastrous and even fatal because of deaths from alcohol poisoning and drunk driving crashes. In July 2008, McCardell organized the Amethyst Initiative, which took its name from the violet-colored gemstone ancient Greeks superstitiously believed could prevent intoxication.

The effort involved college presidents who signed a letter that claimed "twenty-one is not working" and that as a result "a culture of dangerous, clandestine [secret] 'binge-drinking'—often conducted off-campus—has developed." The statement also said that the higher age seemed foolish because "adults under 21 are deemed capable of voting, signing contracts, serving on juries and enlisting in the military, but are told they are not mature enough to have a beer."[77] As of 2018, the heads of 136 universities have signed the statement.

ZERO TOLERANCE

"The problem is the first drink makes the second easier and so on ... Your kids may drink, but they should know what your expectation is; and your expectation should be 'no drinking until 21.'"

–Jeff Levy, whose son died after a college drinking party

Quoted in Susan Larson, "Parents, Teens Discuss Perils of College Drinking Culture," *Burke Patch*, July 26, 2011. burke.patch.com/articles/parents-teens-discuss-perils-of-college-drinking-culture.

The Debate over the Drinking Age

Drinking is an accepted part of college life, even though most students are not old enough to drink legally. A 2016 study from the Center for Behavioral Health Statistics and Quality found that more than one-third of college students between the ages of 18 and 22 had engaged in binge drinking in the month prior to the study, which means they had at least 5 drinks in a session. The study also found that about 10 percent of students had tried alcohol for the first time in college. The ease with which older teenagers obtain alcohol, whether they are in college or not, renders the drinking age of 21 almost meaningless in terms of stopping them from drinking. That reality and the fact that people 18 and older are considered adults in other legal situations, such as voting, makes many people believe the drinking age should be returned to 18 or 19.

However, many others believe it should stay at 21. In a Gallup poll before the minimum drinking age law was signed in 1984, 79 percent of Americans supported raising the drinking age to 21. As of a 2014 Gallup poll, 74 percent of Americans still want to keep the higher drinking age. The poll numbers show the continuing fears Americans have about teenage drinking. An article in the June 2010 edition of the *American Journal of Public Health* supported retaining the drinking age of 21 by citing new knowledge about the dangers of teenage drinking. The article's authors, Henry Wechsler and Toben F. Nelson, wrote,

> *The weight of the scientific evidence, evaluated by many experts and government agencies, demonstrates that the minimum legal drinking age of 21 years is effective public policy for reducing underage drinking and preventing the negative consequences that can result from underage drinking. The evidence suggests that making alcohol more available by reducing the minimum legal drinking age to 18 years will lead to an increase in drinking and related [problems].*[78]

Supporters of lowering the drinking age have argued that if teens drank in public, they could be more easily monitored for consumption, and binge drinking would end. Like Professor Garcia Coll in Puerto Rico, many believe the "European method" of introducing responsible alcohol consumption to children long before their teens—for instance, by giving them a sip of their parents' wine—can reduce alcohol abuse in teens. Studies have been done on this, but the results vary wildly. One study published in 2017, which followed 2,000 Australian teens for 4 years, found that those who were given alcohol by their parents were 3 times less likely to binge drink than those given alcohol by their friends. However, in another Australian study released in 2018, researchers found that children whose parents let them try alcohol were more likely to have problems with alcohol later on because they were more than twice as likely to get it from other sources as well. "There is a view that if parents provide small quantities of alcohol to their teenage children and model low-risk drinking, these children will be less likely to drink in risky ways," said Stuart Kinner of the Murdoch Children's Research Institute, who provided information on the study. "The findings of this study suggest the opposite."[79] At the same time, Kinner noted several limitations of the study; for instance, the participants mostly came from wealthy families, and the teens whose parents gave them alcohol may already have been at risk for problem drinking. More studies will need to be done to see which of these findings is more accurate.

Some studies suggest that if parents give children a little bit of alcohol when they are young, they will be less likely to binge drink when they are older. Other studies suggest the exact opposite.

Additionally, the assumption that Europe has less of a problem with teen drinking overall is false. Based on information from the World Health Organization (WHO), the website *Vox* reported in 2016 that more youth in Europe binge drink, and at higher rates, than their U.S. peers. These trends continue into adulthood, and rates of cirrhosis are much higher for European men than for American men.

Reduced teen drinking or binge drinking may have more to do with social support than early exposure. Kids whose parents take a hard line on drinking, meaning they have a zero-tolerance policy, are less likely to drink as teens. Even when they do drink, teens with strict parental rules are less likely to binge drink. According to *Medical Daily*, "As parents become less likely to discipline their children over alcohol use, they become more likely to grant their children permission to drink. This leads to a breakdown in communication, especially when it comes to the consequence of alcohol use."[80]

Concern About Cars

The strongest argument against lowering the drinking age is the reason Congress originally passed the National Minimum Drinking Age Act—the high number of drunk driving fatalities involving teenagers.

As of 2016, the NHTSA estimates that raising the drinking age to 21 has saved 31,417 lives since 1975 (when some

The Role of Genetics

Research is ongoing into whether specific genes–the carriers of deoxyribonucleic acid (DNA), the material that is passed down from parent to child and determines many of people's physical and mental traits–increase a person's risk for developing an alcohol use disorder. Researchers know there is no one single gene that causes someone to develop this disorder, but they also know genetics are about 50 percent responsible for a person's risk. Other factors include opportunity–if someone never takes a drink, they will never become addicted–and emotional and social factors.

For decades, a myth has persisted that Native Americans are genetically predisposed to alcohol use disorders because they are five times more likely than other ethnicities in the United States to become addicted to alcohol. The reasoning was that they metabolized alcohol differently than other races, and people pointed to the fact that alcohol use disorders became a problem among this group after colonists brought spirits over from Europe. However, recent studies have disproven this myth; Native Americans do not metabolize alcohol any differently, and their higher rate of alcohol use disorders is more likely due to the fact that everyone in their culture suffered a severe trauma when their land was invaded by Europeans. Multiple studies have shown a clear link between trauma and addiction. The effects of colonization, such as increased rates of poverty, persist among many Native American groups today, which is why their rates of alcohol abuse still tend to be higher.

individual states raised their drinking age) by making it harder for teenagers to drink and drive. Ralph Hingson, who heads the NIAAA, opposes a lower drinking age for that reason: "We already did the experiment of lowering the drinking age [to 18 in the 1970s], and traffic crashes went up. I don't think it's a good idea to go back and repeat a policy that made things worse."[81] Hingson is also a member of the National

Advisory Council of MADD, a powerful opponent of lowering the drinking age.

One way to understand what lowering the drinking age in the United States might look like is to see what other countries have done. In 1999, New Zealand lowered its drinking age to 18. The country saw an immediate increase in teen drunk driving. However, even with the drinking age set at 21, the United States still has far more drunk driving crashes than other countries. This may be due to a combination of factors. One is that U.S. roads allow people to reach speeds much greater than the posted speed limit; some countries, such as Sweden, have changed their roads to force people to drive more slowly and have been stricter with enforcing the speed limit. However, this has made the roads less convenient to use, so any similar measures would likely meet strong opposition in the United States.

Other countries also have much stricter drunk driving laws. According to *Newsweek*,

> *Researchers found random breath testing is the single most effective way to reduce deaths related to driving and alcohol. Australia had significant success in lowering road deaths related to alcohol by introducing widespread breath testing and its death rate is now around five fatalities per 100,000 people. In general, other rich countries tend to allow less alcohol in drivers' blood than prevailing [current] limits in the U.S.*[82]

Despite strong opposition, there have been several efforts since 1984 to lower the drinking age, including legislation introduced in a handful of states, including in Wisconsin during the 2017 legislative session. None of the attempts has succeeded, but backers of a lower drinking age keep working toward that goal.

A Nation Divided

Americans will always have strong feelings about alcohol use, no matter what the drinking age is. It can be tough for teens—and even adults—to understand what place alcohol should have in their lives. Gail Gleason Milgram, who has studied alcohol use for decades at Rutgers University, believes that any issue involving alcohol will always be controversial because of the deep, divided feelings Americans have about it:

> *We have inconsistent attitudes and behaviors about drinking, which are more complex and controversial than we like to admit. Despite the general availability of alcohol, the problems associated with its use make us uncomfortable, and we often prefer to ignore them altogether. Alcohol strikes an emotional chord in many of us.*[83]

With this in mind, it is clear that one important key to responsible alcohol use later in life is becoming aware early on of the risks associated with it.

NOTES

Introduction: "I Paid with the Life of a Good Friend"

1. Quoted in Donna St. George, "Teen Driver in Fatal Alcohol-Related Crash Is Sentenced to 18 Months in Jail," *Washington Post*, September 10, 2015. www.washingtonpost.com/local/education/teen-driver-in-fatal-alcohol-related-crash-sentenced-to-18-months-in-jail/2015/09/10/5f871426-57be-11e5-b8c9-944725fcd3b9_story.html.
2. Quoted in St. George, "Teen Driver in Fatal Alcohol-Related Crash."
3. Kenneth P. Moritsugu, "The Surgeon General's Call to Action to Prevent and Reduce Underage Drinking 2007," Washington, DC: U.S. Department of Health and Human Services, 2007, p. 1.

Chapter 1: A Widespread Drug

4. Katherine Ketcham and Nicholas A. Pace, *Teens Under the Influence: The Truth About Kids, Alcohol, and Other Drugs—How to Recognize the Problem and What to Do About It*. New York, NY: Ballantine, 2003, p. 19.
5. Susan Cohen and Daniel Cohen, *A Six-Pack and a Fake I.D.: Teens Look at the Drinking Question*. New York, NY: Evans, 1986, p. 129.
6. Gail Gleason Milgram and the Editors of Consumer Reports Books, *The Facts About Drinking: Coping with Alcohol Use, Abuse, and Alcoholism*. Mount Vernon, NY: Consumers Union of United States, 1990, p. 1.
7. Charles Q. Choi, "Origins of Human Alcohol Consumption Revealed," Live Science, December 1, 2014. www.livescience.com/48958-human-origins-alcohol-consumption.html.

8. Quoted in Wolfgang Schivelbusch, *Tastes of Paradise: A Social History of Spices, Stimulants, and Intoxicants*. New York, NY: Pantheon, 1992, p. 22.
9. Quoted in David T. Courtwright, *Forces of Habit: Drugs and the Making of the Modern World*. Cambridge, MA: Harvard University Press, 2001, p. 72.
10. 1 Timothy 5:23 (New American Standard Bible).
11. Quoted in Sharon V. Salinger, *Taverns and Drinking in Early America*. Baltimore, MD: Johns Hopkins University Press, 2002, p. 137.
12. W. J. Rorabaugh, *The Alcoholic Republic: An American Tradition*. New York, NY: Oxford University Press, 1979, p. 35.
13. Thomas R. Pegram, *Battling Demon Rum: The Struggle for a Dry America, 1800–1933*. Chicago, IL: Dee, 1998, p. 8.
14. Quoted in Salinger, *Taverns and Drinking in Early America*, p. 184.
15. Quoted in C. Furnas, *The Life and Times of the Late Demon Rum*. New York, NY: Putnam's Sons, 1965, p. 35.
16. Quoted in Laurie Davies, "21 Turns 20," *Driven*, Spring 2004, p. 23.
17. Quoted in "Canadian Drinking-Age Laws Have Significant Effect on Deaths Among Young Males," University of Northern British Columbia, March 18, 2014. www.unbc.ca/releases/11685/canadian-drinking-age-laws-have-significant-effect-on-deaths-among-young-males.
18. Ronald Reagan, "Statement on the Presidential Commission on Drunk Driving," Ronald Reagan Presidential Library, April 5, 1983. www.reagan.utexas.edu/archives/speeches/1983/40583c.html.
19. Quoted in Richard L. Madden, "6 Northeast Governors Ask Drinking Age of 21," *New York Times*, 1985. www.nytimes.com/1985/01/31/nyregion/6-northeast-governors-ask-drinking-age-of-21.html.

20. "Drinking and Culture: International Comparisons," Choose Responsibility, accessed on March 28, 2018. www.chooseresponsibility.org/drinking_and_culture/.

Chapter 2: Why People Drink

21. Quoted in Jesse Spero, "Demi Lovato Reveals: I Would 'Smuggle' Cocaine On Planes," *Access Hollywood*, December 10, 2013. www.accessonline.com/articles/demi-lovato-reveals-i-would-smuggle-cocaine-on-planes-exclusive-140900/.

22. Cohen and Cohen, *A Six-Pack and a Fake I.D.*, p. 1.

23. Smokeseek, "A Teen Aged Alcoholic," Experience Project, November 24, 2008. www.experienceproject.com/stories/Am-A-Member-Of-Alcoholics-Anonymous/377009.

24. James B. Jacobs, *Drunk Driving: An American Dilemma*. Chicago, IL: University of Chicago Press, 1989, p. 3.

25. Quoted in John Kreiser, "Teen Drinking Takes Toll on Brain," CBS, February 11, 2006. www.cbsnews.com/stories/2006/07/05/eveningnews/main1778434.shtml.

26. Quoted in Leah Odze Epstein, "An Interview with Alexandra Robbins, Author of 'The Geeks Shall Inherit the Earth: Popularity, Quirk Theory, and Why Outsiders Thrive After High School,'" *Drinking Diaries: From Celebration to Revelation*, April 29, 2011. www.drinkingdiaries.com/2011/04/29/an-interview-on-teen-drinking-with-alexandra-robbins-author-of-the-geeks-shall-inherit-the-earth-popularity-quirk-theory-and-why-outsiders-thrive-after-high-school.

27. Quoted in David E. Gehlke, "Mother, Son Detail Perils of Teen Drinking," *Pittsburgh Tribune Review*, October 12, 2006. www.pittsburghlive.com/x/pittsburghtrib/news/pittsburgh/s_474187.html.

28. Reid K. Hester, "Why Do Teenagers Drink Alcohol?," *Self Help*, April 4, 2009. www.selfhelpmagazine.com/article/teen-alcoholism.

29. Jeff, interview by Michael V. Uschan, July 7, 2011.

30. James R. Milam and Katherine Ketcham, *Under the Influence: A Guide to the Myths and Realities of Alcoholism*. Seattle, WA: Madrona, 1981, p. 16.

31. "Effects at Specific BAC Levels," B.R.A.D.21, accessed on March 28, 2018. www.brad21.org/effects_at_specific_bac.html.

32. "Effects at Specific BAC Levels," B.R.A.D.21.

33. Harry Milt, *Alcoholism, Its Causes and Cure: A New Handbook*. New York, NY: Scribner's Sons, 1976, p. 10.

34. "The Try Guys Test the Legal Alcohol Limit," YouTube video, 7:27, posted by BuzzFeedVideo, December 30, 2014. www.youtube.com/watch?v=QTrqGwj3XpA.

35. "The Try Guys Test the Legal Alcohol Limit," posted by BuzzFeedVideo.

36. "The Try Guys Test the Legal Alcohol Limit," posted by BuzzFeedVideo.

Chapter 3: The Dangers of Underage Drinking

37. Quoted in Kerri Smith, "Sex and Drugs and Self-Control: How the Teen Brain Navigates Risk," *Nature*, February 21, 2018. www.nature.com/articles/d41586-018-02170-3.

38. "Teen Traffic Fatalities Increase During Summer: Students Are Out of School and Driving More," Virginia Department of Motor Vehicles, July 16, 2009. www.dmv.virginia.gov/safety/#news/news.asp?id=5598.

39. "Interview: Deborah Yurgelun-Todd," PBS *Frontline: Inside the Teenage Brain*, accessed on March 28, 2018. www.pbs.org/wgbh/pages/frontline/shows/teenbrain/interviews/todd.html.

40. Quoted in Barbara Strauch, *The Primal Teen: What the New Discoveries About the Teenage Brain Tell Us About Our Kids*. New York, NY: Doubleday, 2003, p. 179.

41. Ketcham and Pace, *Teens Under the Influence*, p. 45.

42. Quoted in Kelly Adams, "Driving While a Male Teen," *Vancouver Columbian*, September 24, 2006, p. 1.

43. Mike, interview by Michael V. Uschan, August 16, 2011.

44. Quoted in Alan B. Goldberg, "Drunken Driver Grants Prison Interview, Shares the Emotional Pain of Killing Her Best Friend," ABC News, June 3, 2009. abcnews.go.com/2020/story?id=7726708&page=1.

45. Madison Park, "Ethan Couch of 'Affluenza' Case Released from Jail," CNN, April 2, 2018. www.cnn.com/2018/04/02/us/ethan-couch-affluenza-jail-release/index.html.

46. Quoted in Park, "Ethan Couch of 'Affluenza' Case Released from Jail."

47. Jack, interview by Michael V. Uschan, August 5, 2011.

48. Greg, interview by Michael V. Uschan, August 5, 2011.

49. Quoted in Rebecca Lurye, "At Least 90 Hospitalized, 50 Charged with Underage Drinking at Hartford 'Hot Jam' Concert," *Hartford Courant*, July 22, 2017. www.courant.com/breaking-news/hc-hartford-hotjam-concert-drinking-0723-20170722-story.html.

50. "College Drinking Is a Culture," *A Call to Action: Changing the Culture of Drinking at U.S. Colleges*, National Institute on Alcohol Abuse and Alcoholism, April 2002, p. 1. www.collegedrinkingprevention.gov/niaaacollegematerials/taskforce/Intro_00.aspx.

51. Simon Lenton, "Why Do Our Friends Want Us to Drink and Dislike It When We Don't?," The Conversation, December 28, 2016. theconversation.com/why-do-our-friends-want-us-to-drink-and-dislike-it-when-we-dont-68430.

52. "The Effects of Combining Alcohol with Other Drugs," University of Michigan, accessed on April 2, 2018. uhs.umich.edu/combine.

53. Sarah Hepola, "Ask a Former Drunk: When Do You Know You Have a Problem?," *Jezebel*, June 7, 2016. jezebel.com/ask-a-former-drunk-when-do-you-know-you-have-a-problem-1780859204.

54. Quoted in Michael E. Miller, "'A Steep Price to Pay for 20 Minutes of Action': Dad Defends Stanford Sex Offender," *Washington Post*, June 6, 2016. www.washingtonpost.com/news/morning-mix/wp/2016/06/06/a-steep-price-to-pay-for-20-minutes-of-action-dad-defends-stanford-sex-offender/.

55. Quoted in Lauren R. Taylor and Jessica Raven, "Alcohol Isn't the Cause of Campus Sexual Assault. Men Are," *Washington Post*, June 10, 2016. www.washingtonpost.com/posteverything/wp/2016/06/10/alcohol-isnt-what-causes-campus-sexual-assault-men-are/?utm_term=.86384b364561.

56. Quoted in Jeff Mosier, "Date Rape Warning Given to Arlington Teens: Link Between Drinking, Rape Stressed After Possible Assaults," *Dallas Morning News*, September 28, 2006, p. 1.

57. Taylor and Raven, "Alcohol Isn't the Cause."

58. Taylor and Raven, "Alcohol Isn't the Cause."

59. Quoted in Katy Butler, "The Grim Neurology of Teenage Drinking," *New York Times*, July 5, 2006. www.nytimes.com/2006/07/04/health/04teen.html.

60. *The Surgeon General's Call to Action To Prevent and Reduce Underage Drinking: A Guide to Action for Communities*, U.S. Department of Health and Human Services, Office of the Surgeon General, 2007. www.surgeongeneral.gov/library/calls/underage-drinking-community-guide.pdf.

61. Karen Opas, "What It's Like to Be an Alcoholic," *Business Insider*, February 13, 2014. www.businessinsider.com/heres-what-its-like-to-be-an-alcoholic-2014-2.

Chapter 4: Choosing Wisely: Prevention

62. Quoted in Kristen Thometz, "New Initiative Aims to Reduce Alcohol Use in Chicago Teens," *Chicago Tonight*, WTTW, March 12, 2018. chicagotonight.wttw.com/2018/03/12/new-initiative-aims-reduce-alcohol-use-chicago-teens.

63. Quoted in WSFA 12 News Staff, "Panama City Beach Spring Break Alcohol Ban Starts," ABC 27 WTXL, March 11, 2018. www.wtxl.com/news/panama-city-beach-spring-break-alcohol-ban-starts/article_dae9a946-2555-11e8-8176-2f0097f1beaa.html.

64. Quoted in Steele Cameron, "Dramatization at Alexandria High School Illustrates Dangers of Teen Drinking, Driving," *Anniston (AL) Star*, March 27, 2011, p. 1.

65. Quoted in Emma Young, "How Iceland Got Teens to Say No to Drugs," *The Atlantic*, January 19, 2017. www.theatlantic.com/health/archive/2017/01/teens-drugs-iceland/513668/.

66. Quoted in "Grantee Highlights for the STOP Program," SAMHSA News, March/April 2010. www.samhsa.gov/samhsanewsletter/Volume_18_Number_2/Grantees.aspx.

67. Quoted in "Grantee Highlights for the STOP Program," SAMHSA News.

68. Quoted in Devin Leith-Yessian, "Youth Coalition Uses Stickers to Combat Underage Drinking," *U.S. News & World Report*, April 2, 2018. www.usnews.com/news/best-states/connecticut/articles/2018-04-02/youth-coalition-uses-stickers-to-combat-underage-drinking.

69. Quoted in Bonnie Delaney, "Underage Drinking: Towns Take a Stand," *Asbury Park Press*, August 23, 2011. www.app.com/article/20110823/NJNEWS/308230016/Underage-drinking-Towns-take-a-stand.

70. *Mean Girls*, directed by Mark Waters (Los Angeles, CA: Paramount Studios, 2004), DVD.

71. Petula Dvorak, "Parents Who Host Teen Drinking Parties: Not Cool, Not Smart, but They Do It Anyway," *Washington Post*, November 12, 2015. www.washingtonpost.com/local/parents-who-host-teen-drinking-parties-not-cool-not-smart-but-they-do-it-anyway/2015/11/12/a4a5a05e-8937-11e5-9a07-453018f9a0ec_story.html?utm_term=.18d6522d4e71.

72. Jeanne Mejeur, "Young Drunk Drivers," State Legislatures, April 2005, p. 15.

73. Cohen and Cohen, *A Six-Pack and a Fake I.D.*, p. 9.

74. Quoted in Matthew Sturdevant, "New Survey Says Few Teens Drink and Drive on Prom Night," *Hartford Courant*, April 18, 2011. blogs.courant.com/connecticut_insurance/2011/04/new-survey-says-few-teens-drin.html.

Chapter 5: The Age of Experience: 18 or 21?

75. Quoted in Barbara Kantrowitz, "Toddler Served Margarita in a Sippy Cup," *Newsweek*, June 24, 2007. www.newsweek.com/toddler-served-margarita-sippy-cup-101963.

76. Quoted in Sean Flynn, "Should the Drinking Age Be Lowered?," *Parade*, August 12, 2007. www.parade.com/articles/editions/2007/edition_08-12-2007/Teen_Drinking?prnt=1.

77. "Statement," Amethyst Initiative, accessed on April 4, 2018. www.theamethystinitiative.org/statement/.

78. Quoted in Barbara Kantrowitz and Anne Underwood, "The Teen Drinking Dilemma," *Newsweek*, June 25, 2007, p. 36.

79. Quoted in Lisa Rapaport, "Letting Teens Imbibe a Little to Teach Responsible Drinking Seems to Backfire, Study Finds," *Washington Post*, February 19, 2018. www.washingtonpost.com/national/health-science/letting-teens-imbibe-a-little-to-teach-responsible-drinking-seems-to-backfire-study-finds/2018/02/16/95190c12-128c-11e8-957029c98305 35e5_story.html?utm_term=.79da58ad9814.

80. Justin Caba, "Adolescent Alcohol Use: Parents' Attitude Toward Alcohol Often Predicts if Their Children Will Drink," *Medical Daily*, January 9, 2015. www.medicaldaily.com/adolescent-alcohol-use-parents-attitude-toward-alcohol-often-predicts-if-their-317112.

81. Quoted in Flynn, "Should the Drinking Age Be Lowered?"

82. Serge Bloch, "You Drive Like an American!," *Newsweek*, March 27, 2014. www.newsweek.com/2014/04/04/you-drive-american-248061.html.

83. Milgram and the Editors of Consumer Reports Books, *The Facts About Drinking*, p. 1.

DISCUSSION QUESTIONS

Chapter 1: A Widespread Drug

1. When you think of drugs, do you also think of alcohol? Why or why not?
2. What do you think the minimum drinking age should be?
3. Describe your attitude toward alcohol. What factors have influenced your views?

Chapter 2: Why People Drink

1. Have you tried or thought about trying alcohol? Why or why not?
2. Do you believe drinking is something all teens do?
3. What are some silly or dangerous things you have heard of people doing when they are drunk? Do you think they would have done them if they had been sober?

Chapter 3: The Dangers of Underage Drinking

1. Do you believe teenagers have more difficulty than adults with assessing risk?
2. Do you know anyone who has chosen to drive after drinking? Has this affected how you view this issue?
3. Why is it important for people to take responsibility for the things they do when they have been drinking?

Chapter 4: Choosing Wisely: Prevention

1. Would a program such as Youth in Europe, with its curfews and parental involvement, work in the United States? Explain your reasoning for the answer you gave.
2. If your school held a mock fatal crash event, how do you think it would affect your views on drunk driving?
3. Explain social hosting ordinances or laws. Do you believe they are necessary?

Chapter 5: The Age of Experience: 18 or 21?

1. How have the adults around you influenced your views on alcohol?
2. What do you think is a good drinking policy for parents to set for their teens?
3. After reading this chapter, has your opinion about what the minimum drinking age should be changed or stayed the same as the answer you gave in Chapter 1?

ORGANIZATIONS TO CONTACT

Al-Anon Family Groups
1600 Corporate Landing Pkwy.
Virginia Beach, VA 23454
(757) 563-1600
wso@al-anon.org
al-anon.org

Al-Anon Family Groups, made up of Al-Anon and Alateen, are support groups that provide comfort, understanding, and encouragement for the spouses, children, and other relatives and friends of people with an alcohol use disorder. Al-Anon is different than Alcoholics Anonymous (AA), which provides support and recovery for people with an alcohol use disorder.

Foundation for Advancing Alcohol Responsibility
2345 Crystal Drive, Suite 710
Arlington, VA 22202
(202) 637-0077
www.responsibility.org

This nonprofit organization focuses on stopping underage drinking and drunk driving by providing information and public messaging campaigns.

Substance Abuse and Mental Health Services Administration (SAMHSA)
5600 Fishers Lane
Rockville, MD 20847
(877) 726-4727
samhsa.gov

SAMHSA is an agency within the U.S. Department of Health and Human Services that provides information from the federal government about alcohol, substance abuse, and mental health.

Students Against Destructive Decisions (SADD)
1440 G Street
Washington, D.C. 20005
(508) 481-3568
www.sadd.org

Formerly known as Students Against Drunk Driving, this peer-to-peer education, prevention, and activism organization works to stop teens from drinking and doing other things that will harm them. The group has thousands of local chapters throughout the United States, most of which function as school clubs.

Teen Addiction Anonymous
P.O. Box 20524
Phoenix, AZ 85036
www.teenaddictionanonymous.org

Teen Addiction Anonymous offers programs created by teens for young adults between the ages of 13 and 24. Its website includes the 12 recovery steps for teens, stories of recovery, curriculums for schools, publications, and a self-help test.

FOR MORE INFORMATION

Books

Covey, Sean. *The 6 Most Important Decisions You'll Ever Make: A Guide for Teens*. New York, NY: Touchstone, 2017.
The author helps teens learn how to navigate interpersonal relationships, substance use and abuse, and doing well in school.

Esherick, Joan. *Drug- & Alcohol-Related Health Issues*. Broomall, PA: Mason Crest Publishers, 2014.
Esherick's book provides important information on the severe health issues that heavy drinking over a long period of time can cause.

Ketcham, Katherine, and Nicholas A. Pace. *Teens Under the Influence: The Truth About Kids, Alcohol, and Other Drugs—How to Recognize the Problem and What to Do About It*. New York, NY: Ballantine, 2003.
This book includes many interviews with teenagers who have gotten into trouble by drinking.

Landau, Jennifer. *Helping a Friend with an Alcohol Problem*. New York, NY: Rosen Publishing, 2017.
People who have an alcohol use disorder need the support of their loved ones to help them overcome it. This book gives tips on how to help a friend who is struggling with this disorder.

Parks, Peggy. *The Dangers of Alcohol*. San Diego, CA: ReferencePoint Press, 2017.
This book includes information about treatment and recovery for an alcohol use disorder.

Websites

Choose Responsibility
www.chooseresponsibility.org
This nonprofit organization is focused on responsible drinking initiatives and providing information for and against a change in the minimum drinking age.

MedlinePlus: Underage Drinking
medlineplus.gov/underagedrinking.html
This website by the National Library of Medicine and National Institutes of Health offers information on the medical effects, consequences, and prevention of underage drinking.

National Institute on Alcohol Abuse and Alcoholism (NIAAA)
www.niaaa.nih.gov
A division of the government's National Institutes of Health, this website provides statistics, research, news, and other information on drinking in the United States.

NIDA for Teens: Alcohol
teens.drugabuse.gov/drug-facts/alcohol
This website has information for young adults about the consequences of underage drinking and how to help someone who is suffering from alcohol poisoning.

Partnership for Drug-Free Kids
www.drugfree.org
This website has information about alcohol and drug abuse prevention, intervention, treatment, and recovery for teens and young adults.

TeensHealth: Alcohol
kidshealth.org/en/teens/alcohol.html
This website has a thorough explanation of alcohol, its effects, and the risks of drinking for teens.

INDEX

PICTURE CREDITS

Cover Philippe Lissac/GODONG/Corbis Documentary/Getty Images; p. 7 Tom Wang/Shutterstock.com; p. 8 Image Source/Getty Images; p. 12 Africa Studio/Shutterstock.com; p. 14 National Geographic Creative/Alamy Stock Photo; p. 15 ERIC FEFERBERG/AFP/Getty Images; p. 16 Stock Montage/Getty Images; p. 19 © iStockphoto.com/400tmax; p. 22 Larry Burrows/Time & Life Pictures/Getty Images; p. 23 Universal Images Group North America LLC/Alamy Stock Photo; p. 25 Jupiterimages/Photolibrary/Getty Images; p. 26 Rodrigo Varela/Getty Images for Fontainebleau Miami Beach; p. 28 imageBROKER/Alamy Stock Photo; p. 30 Moviestore collection Ltd/Alamy Stock Photo; p. 31 Sonja Flemming/CBS via Getty Images; p. 33 PhotoMediaGroup/Shutterstock.com; p. 35 (top) JohanKalen/Shutterstock.com; p. 35 (bottom) Hana Socho/Shutterstock.com; p. 38 Jan H Andersen/Shutterstock.com; p. 39 Daniel Zuchnik/WireImage/Getty Images; p. 41 eranicle/Shutterstock.com; p. 42 Jack Dagley Photography/Shutterstock.com; p. 46 sungju kim/Shutterstock.com; p. 48 Max Faulkner/Fort Worth Star-Telegram/TNS via Getty Images; p. 53 michelaubryphoto/Shutterstock.com; p. 55 Photographee.eu/Shutterstock.com; p. 57 Fotos593/Shutterstock.com; p. 66 Gavin Quirke/Lonely Planet Images/Getty Images; p. 68 okili77/Shutterstock.com; p. 70 LightField Studios/Shutterstock.com; p. 71 nikamo/Shutterstock.com; p. 73 Hemant Mehta/Getty Images; p. 77 William G Forbes/Shutterstock.com; p. 80 Jon Feingersh/Blend Images/Getty Images.

ABOUT THE AUTHOR

Allison Krumsiek is an author and poet living outside Washington, D.C. Her previous books include titles from the Hot Topics and People in the News series from Lucent Press. She also writes for a number of organizations, including nonprofits and the federal government. When she is not writing or editing, she can be found reading books or fearlessly defending her field hockey goal, but never at the same time.